While every precaution has been taken in the preparation of this book, the publisher assumes no responsibility for errors or omissions, or for damages resulting from the use of the information contained herein.

DIGITAL WELLNESS FOR BUSY PROFESSIONALS: HOW TO MAINTAIN HEALTH AND PRODUCTIVITY IN A HIGH-STRESS JOB

First edition. May 17, 2024.

Copyright © 2024 Eric Porres.

Written by Eric Porres.

Table of Contents

Copyright Page 1
Introduction: Embracing Digital Wellness and Productivity 5
Chapter 1: Mastering the Art of Digital Detox.................................12
Chapter 2: Microbreaks: Your Secret Productivity Booster............20
Chapter 3: Perfecting Screen Brightness for Health......................27
Chapter 4: Radical Digital Minimalism..34
Chapter 5: Building the Ultimate Distraction-Free Workspace 41
Chapter 6: Blue Light Filters: Why You Need Them 49
Chapter 7: Enforcing Tech Boundaries 57
Chapter 8: Focus-Boosting Apps You Must Try.............................64
Chapter 9: Digital Ergonomics: The New Essentials 72
Chapter 10: Eye Strain No More: Top Techniques 80
Chapter 11: Transforming Email Management 88
Chapter 12: Morning Routines for Digital Productivity...................95
Chapter 13: The Profound Effects of a Social Media Detox........103
Chapter 14: Extreme Time-Blocking for Focus 111
Chapter 15: Wearables: Your Wellness Allies 119
Chapter 16: Decluttering Your Digital Life 127
Chapter 17: Stress Relief Through Digital Tools 135
Chapter 18: Harmonizing Screen and Offline Time.....................142
Chapter 19: Mastering Do Not Disturb Mode 149
Chapter 20: Remote Work Wellness Habits 156
Chapter 21: Digital Day Mindfulness Practices 164
Chapter 22: Technology for Enhancing Sleep.............................171
Chapter 23: Practicing Comprehensive Digital Mindfulness........178
Chapter 24: Designing Tech-Free Sanctuaries 186
Chapter 25: Conducting Healthy Online Meetings 194
Sources..201
Sign up for Eric Porres's Mailing List 205

Introduction: Embracing Digital Wellness and Productivity

In today's fast-paced digital world, technology is an integral part of our daily lives. From smartphones and laptops to wearable devices and smart home gadgets, we are constantly connected. These advancements offer numerous benefits, enabling us to work efficiently, stay connected with loved ones, and access information at our fingertips. However, they also come with challenges. Prolonged screen time, digital distractions, and the blurring of boundaries between work and personal life can lead to stress, burnout, and decreased productivity.

The Impact of Technology on Our Lives

The proliferation of digital devices has transformed the way we live and work. On one hand, technology has revolutionized communication, making it easier than ever to connect with people across the globe. On the other hand, it has introduced new stressors, such as information overload, constant notifications, and the pressure to be always available. Understanding the dual nature of technology is the first step towards achieving digital wellness.

The Benefits of Technology

Technology has undoubtedly brought about significant advancements in various aspects of our lives:

- **Enhanced Communication**: Platforms like email, social media, and messaging apps have made it possible to stay in touch with family, friends, and colleagues, regardless of geographic location. According to a study by Pew Research Center, over 80% of Americans believe that technology has improved their ability to communicate.

- **Increased Productivity**: Tools and applications designed for project management, collaboration, and automation have streamlined workflows and improved efficiency. The McKinsey Global Institute reports that productivity tools can boost efficiency by up to 25%.

- **Access to Information**: The internet provides instant access to a vast amount of information, empowering individuals to learn new skills, stay informed, and make data-driven decisions. A study by the World Bank highlights that access to information can significantly enhance education and economic opportunities.

- **Convenience and Comfort**: Smart home devices, wearable technology, and e-commerce platforms have made daily tasks more convenient, enhancing our overall quality of life. The International Data Corporation (IDC) predicts that the smart home market will continue to grow, reaching $222 billion by 2025.

The Challenges of Technology

Despite these benefits, the pervasive use of technology also presents several challenges:

- **Digital Overload**: Constant exposure to digital content can lead to information overload, making it difficult to process and retain information. The American Psychological Association notes that information overload can contribute to increased stress and anxiety.

- **Decreased Attention Span**: The rapid pace of digital interactions can shorten our attention span and reduce our ability to engage in deep, focused work. A study by Microsoft found that the average human attention span has decreased from 12 seconds in 2000 to 8 seconds in 2013.

- **Mental Health Issues**: Excessive screen time and social media use have been linked to anxiety, depression, and other mental health issues. Research published in the

Journal of Social and Clinical Psychology found that reducing social media use can significantly improve mental health.

- **Physical Health Concerns**: Prolonged use of digital devices can contribute to physical ailments such as eye strain, poor posture, and repetitive strain injuries. The Vision Council reports that over 60% of Americans experience symptoms of digital eye strain.

- **Work-Life Imbalance**: The blurring of boundaries between work and personal life can lead to burnout and reduced overall well-being. The Harvard Business Review emphasizes the importance of setting boundaries to maintain a healthy work-life balance.

Why Digital Wellness Matters

Digital wellness refers to the intentional use of technology in a way that promotes physical, mental, and emotional health. It involves managing screen time, setting healthy boundaries, and creating a balanced relationship with digital devices. As our reliance on technology grows, prioritizing digital wellness becomes crucial for maintaining overall health and achieving a sustainable work-life balance.

The Concept of Digital Detox

A digital detox involves taking a break from digital devices to reduce stress and improve mental well-being. This practice allows individuals to reconnect with the physical world, engage in offline activities, and reduce the negative impacts of constant connectivity. Research has shown that digital detoxes can lead to significant improvements in mood, focus, and overall quality of life. Dr. Nicholas Kardaras, author of *Glow Kids*, emphasizes that taking regular breaks from screens is essential for maintaining mental health.

The Role of Ergonomics

Digital wellness also encompasses the physical aspect of interacting with technology. Ergonomics, the science of designing and arranging workplaces, products, and systems to fit the people who use them, plays a critical role in preventing physical strain and promoting comfort. Proper ergonomic practices can help reduce the risk of musculoskeletal disorders and enhance productivity. The Occupational Safety and Health Administration (OSHA) provides guidelines for setting up ergonomic workspaces to prevent common injuries.

The Scope of This Ebook

This ebook covers a wide range of topics related to digital wellness and productivity. Each chapter delves into a specific aspect of digital life, offering actionable tips and strategies backed by scientific research and expert recommendations. Whether you're looking to implement a digital detox, optimize your workspace, or enhance your focus with mindfulness practices, this guide has you covered.

Topics Explored in This Ebook

- **Mastering the Art of Digital Detox**: Learn why digital detoxes are essential and how to implement them effectively.

- **Microbreaks: Your Secret Productivity Booster**: Discover the power of short, frequent breaks to enhance focus and reduce fatigue.

- **Perfecting Screen Brightness for Health**: Understand the importance of optimal screen brightness for reducing eye strain and improving comfort.

- **Radical Digital Minimalism**: Dive into strategies to declutter your digital life and focus on what truly matters.

- **Enforcing Tech Boundaries**: Set and maintain healthy boundaries with technology to improve work-life balance.

- **Using Apps to Improve Focus**: Explore top apps designed to enhance your focus and productivity.

- **Building the Ultimate Distraction-Free Workspace**: Create a workspace that minimizes distractions and maximizes productivity.

- **Blue Light Filters: Why You Need Them**: Learn how to protect your eyes and improve sleep quality by using blue light filters.

- **Digital Ergonomics: The New Essentials**: Set up an ergonomic workspace to reduce physical strain and enhance productivity.

- **Eye Strain No More: Top Techniques**: Implement techniques to reduce eye strain and maintain eye health in the digital age.

- **Transforming Email Management**: Revolutionize the way you handle emails with strategies for inbox zero, prioritization, and efficient communication.

- **Morning Routines for Digital Productivity**: Start your day with routines that enhance digital productivity and set you up for success.

- **The Profound Effects of a Social Media Detox**: Discover the mental and emotional benefits of taking a break from social media.

- **Extreme Time-Blocking for Focus**: Master the art of time-blocking to organize your day and achieve more.

- **Wearables: Your Wellness Allies**: Utilize wearables to track and improve your health and wellness.

- **Decluttering Your Digital Life**: Simplify and organize your digital environment by decluttering your devices, files, and apps.

- **Stress Relief Through Digital Tools**: Leverage technology to manage stress with apps and tools designed for relaxation and mindfulness.

- **Harmonizing Screen and Offline Time**: Find the perfect balance between screen time and offline activities to enhance your overall well-being.

- **Mastering Do Not Disturb Mode**: Use the Do Not Disturb feature on your devices to minimize interruptions and stay focused.

- **Remote Work Wellness Habits**: Develop healthy habits for remote work, including ergonomic setups, regular breaks, and maintaining work-life balance.

- **Digital Day Mindfulness Practices**: Integrate mindfulness into your daily digital routine to reduce stress and increase focus.

- **Technology for Enhancing Sleep**: Use technology to improve your sleep quality with apps and devices designed for better sleep hygiene and relaxation.

- **Practicing Comprehensive Digital Mindfulness**: Embrace digital mindfulness to navigate the digital world with awareness and intention.

- **Designing Tech-Free Sanctuaries**: Create tech-free zones in your home or workspace to promote relaxation and focus.

- **Conducting Healthy Online Meetings**: Learn best practices for productive and less draining virtual meetings.

What You'll Learn

By reading this ebook, you'll gain:

- **Actionable Strategies**: Practical tips and techniques to improve your digital wellness and productivity.

- **Expert Insights**: Knowledge from leading experts in digital health, psychology, and productivity.

- **Comprehensive Coverage**: A holistic approach to managing various aspects of digital life, from screen brightness to online meeting etiquette.

- **Real-Life Examples**: Case studies and personal stories to illustrate the application of strategies in real-world scenarios.

How to Use This Ebook

This ebook is designed to be a comprehensive yet flexible guide. You can read it from cover to cover or jump to specific chapters that address your current needs and interests. Each chapter stands alone, providing valuable insights and practical advice that you can implement immediately.

Reading Tips

- **Take Notes**: Jot down key points and actionable tips that resonate with you.

- **Reflect and Apply**: Reflect on the strategies and how they can be applied to your unique situation.

- **Share and Discuss**: Share insights with friends, family, or colleagues and discuss how you can support each other in achieving digital wellness.

My Commitment to Your Well-Being

As the leader of Logitech's innovation group and a former CMO of several successful tech companies, I have witnessed firsthand the profound impact of technology on our lives. My team and I are dedicated to helping you develop smarter wellness habits and achieve a balanced, productive digital lifestyle. This ebook is a culmination of my research, expertise, and passion for promoting digital well-being.

I hope you find this guide valuable and inspiring. By embracing the principles and practices outlined in this ebook, you can take control of your digital life, enhance your productivity, and improve your overall well-being. Let's embark on this journey together towards a healthier, more balanced relationship with technology.

Chapter 1: Mastering the Art of Digital Detox

The Silent Stream

A student approached the teacher and asked, "How can I find clarity in a world full of digital noise?"

The teacher led the student to a stream and said, "Sit here and listen to the water."

The student listened intently but soon grew restless and said, "I hear the water, but my mind is still noisy."

The teacher picked up a stone and threw it into the stream. "What do you see?" the teacher asked.

The student replied, "I see ripples disturbing the water."

The teacher nodded, "And what happens to the ripples?"

The student watched as the ripples gradually faded away, leaving the water clear and calm again. "They disappear, and the water returns to stillness," the student observed.

The teacher smiled, "Just as the water becomes clear when left undisturbed, your mind finds clarity when you step away from the digital noise. Embrace the stillness and let the ripples of distraction fade."

The student understood and began practicing regular digital detoxes, finding clarity and peace in the stillness.

Introduction

In today's hyper-connected world, the constant barrage of digital information can be overwhelming. Our devices, while incredibly useful, can also contribute to stress, anxiety, and a lack of focus. This chapter explores the concept of a digital detox, providing insights into why it's necessary and how to implement it effectively.

Understanding the Concept

A digital detox refers to a period during which an individual refrains from using digital devices such as smartphones, computers, and tablets. The purpose is to reduce stress and improve mental well-being by disconnecting from the constant stream of digital information.

Dr. Nicholas Kardaras, author of *Glow Kids: How Screen Addiction Is Hijacking Our Kids—and How to Break the Trance*, explains that digital screens can have a profound impact on our brains, similar to addictive substances. The overuse of technology can lead to changes in brain chemistry, affecting attention, behavior, and emotional regulation. Kardaras highlights that the brain's reward system can be hijacked by the instant gratification provided by digital devices, leading to compulsive use and addiction-like symptoms.

Dr. Kimberly Young, founder of the Center for Internet Addiction, has conducted extensive research on the effects of excessive internet use and advocates for regular digital detoxes to maintain mental health. Young's research indicates that internet addiction can lead to various psychological issues, including depression, anxiety, and social isolation. By taking a break from digital devices, individuals can reset their brain's reward system and reduce the negative impacts of excessive screen time.

Expert Insights and Research

Research published in the *Journal of Behavioral Addictions* highlights that excessive screen time can lead to symptoms similar to substance addiction, including withdrawal, tolerance, and negative impacts on daily life. Professor Mark Griffiths from Nottingham Trent University has extensively studied digital addiction and supports the idea of digital detoxes to mitigate these effects. Griffiths' research emphasizes that digital addiction shares many characteristics with other behavioral addictions, such as gambling and gaming.

Sherry Turkle, a professor at MIT and author of *Alone Together*, discusses how constant connectivity can lead to a sense of isolation and reduced quality of interpersonal relationships. Turkle's studies show that while technology allows for more frequent communication, it often lacks the depth and richness of face-to-face interactions. This superficial communication can contribute to feelings of loneliness and disconnection.

The American Psychological Association also emphasizes the importance of taking breaks from digital devices to prevent burnout and maintain mental health. In their guidelines for managing screen time, the APA suggests that regular breaks from screens can improve cognitive function, enhance mood, and increase overall well-being. A study conducted by the APA found that participants who engaged in a digital detox reported significant improvements in their overall mood and well-being. The study highlighted that even short-term breaks from digital devices could reduce stress and improve focus.

Additionally, research from the *Journal of Cyberpsychology, Behavior, and Social Networking* found that individuals who took regular digital detoxes experienced lower levels of anxiety and higher levels of life satisfaction. The study suggests that digital detoxes can help individuals regain control over their technology use, leading to more intentional and mindful interactions with digital devices.

Practical Steps and Tips

1. Set Clear Goals Before beginning a digital detox, it's essential to set clear and achievable goals. Determine what you want to achieve, whether it's reducing stress, improving focus, or reconnecting with the physical world. Setting specific objectives will help you stay motivated throughout the detox process. For example, you might aim to spend more time outdoors, engage in physical activities, or connect with family and friends in person.

2. Establish Boundaries Create specific times or days when you will avoid using digital devices. Inform friends and family about your detox to manage their expectations and gain their support. Establishing boundaries is crucial for maintaining discipline and ensuring the success of your detox. For instance, you could designate weekends or evenings as tech-free times. According to Dr. Larry Rosen, author of *The Distracted Mind: Ancient Brains in a High-Tech World*, setting boundaries is key to achieving a balanced digital life.

3. Find Alternatives Replace screen time with activities you enjoy, such as reading, exercising, or spending time with loved ones. Engaging in meaningful offline activities can help fill the void left by reduced screen time and enhance your overall well-being. Activities like hiking, painting, cooking, or playing a musical instrument can provide a fulfilling alternative to digital engagement.

4. Use Tools to Limit Access Utilize apps and tools to limit your screen usage. Apps like Freedom and StayFocusd can block access to digital devices during designated times, helping you stay on track with your detox goals. A study in the *Journal of Behavioral Addictions* suggests that these tools can effectively reduce the temptation to use screens. Additionally, setting up app usage limits and enabling "Do Not Disturb" modes can help manage distractions.

5. Reflect on the Benefits After completing your detox, take time to reflect on how you feel. Have you noticed improvements in your mood, focus, or overall well-being? Research from the *American Psychological Association* suggests that reflecting on positive outcomes can reinforce the benefits and encourage continued mindful use of digital devices. Journaling about your experiences and the changes you've noticed can provide valuable insights and motivation to maintain healthier habits.

6. Gradual Reintroduction When reintroducing digital devices into your routine, do so gradually. Start with essential tasks and slowly add other activities as needed. Dr. Larry Rosen, a psychologist specializing in technology use, advises a controlled reintroduction to maintain the benefits of the detox. For instance, you might initially limit your screen time to a few hours a day and gradually increase it while monitoring its impact on your well-being.

7. Create Long-Term Habits Develop long-term habits to ensure ongoing digital wellness. This could include regular digital detoxes, setting daily screen time limits, or establishing tech-free zones in your home. The *Pew Research Center* suggests that consistent habits can lead to sustained improvements in well-being. Implementing practices like "tech-free Sundays" or "device-free dinners" can help create a lasting balance between digital and offline life.

Additional Strategies for a Successful Digital Detox

1. Digital Declutter Just as physical clutter can affect your mental state, digital clutter can also contribute to stress. Take time to declutter your digital space by organizing files, deleting unnecessary apps, and cleaning up your email inbox. Marie Kondo's principles of tidying up can be applied to digital spaces, helping you create a more organized and calming digital environment.

2. Engage in Mindfulness Practices Incorporate mindfulness practices into your daily routine to help manage stress and improve focus. Techniques such as meditation, deep breathing exercises, and yoga can enhance your ability to stay present and reduce the urge to constantly check your devices. The *Journal of Psychosomatic Research* highlights that mindfulness practices can significantly reduce anxiety and improve mental clarity.

3. Schedule Tech-Free Activities Plan and schedule activities that do not involve technology. Whether it's a weekend camping trip, a visit to a museum, or a day spent gardening, having tech-free activities on your calendar can provide a much-needed break from screens and offer new experiences.

4. Seek Social Support Share your digital detox goals with friends and family, and seek their support. Engaging in a digital detox together can strengthen relationships and provide mutual encouragement. According to Dr. Emma Seppälä, author of *The Happiness Track*, social support is crucial for achieving and maintaining personal goals.

Do's and Don'ts of Digital Detox
Do's:

• **Do set clear and realistic goals**: Know what you want to achieve with your digital detox.

• **Do inform others**: Let friends, family, and colleagues know about your detox to gain their support.

• **Do find enjoyable alternatives**: Engage in offline activities that you love.

• **Do use technology to limit technology**: Utilize apps to help you stay on track.

• **Do reflect on your progress**: Regularly assess how you feel during and after the detox.

• **Do gradually reintroduce technology**: Slowly add digital activities back into your routine.

• **Do create long-term habits**: Develop ongoing practices to maintain digital wellness.

Don'ts:

- **Don't set unrealistic expectations**: Understand that it might take time to see significant changes.

- **Don't go it alone**: Seek support from others who understand your goals.

- **Don't replace one screen with another**: Avoid substituting your phone with a computer or TV.

- **Don't ignore the benefits**: Acknowledge and appreciate the positive changes you experience.

- **Don't rush the process**: Allow yourself time to adjust to the changes.

- **Don't neglect offline interactions**: Prioritize face-to-face interactions over digital ones.

- **Don't forget to celebrate small victories**: Recognize and celebrate your progress.

FAQ: Digital Detox

Q: **How long should a digital detox last?** A: The duration of a digital detox can vary based on individual needs. It can range from a few hours to several days or even weeks. Start with shorter periods and gradually increase the duration as needed.

Q: **What if I need to use my phone for work or emergencies?** A: Set specific times when you can check your phone for work-related tasks or emergencies. Use features like "Do Not Disturb" to minimize distractions and prioritize essential tasks.

Q: **How can I stay motivated during a digital detox?** A: Set clear goals, track your progress, and reward yourself for meeting milestones. Engaging in enjoyable offline activities and seeking support from friends and family can also help maintain motivation.

Q: **Can children benefit from a digital detox?** A: Yes, children can benefit significantly from digital detoxes. It can help improve their attention span, reduce exposure to harmful content, and encourage healthier habits. Involve children in offline activities and set a positive example by participating in the detox with them.

Q: What are some signs that I need a digital detox? A: Common signs include feeling overwhelmed by constant notifications, experiencing anxiety or stress related to digital devices, difficulty focusing, and neglecting offline relationships and activities. If you notice these signs, it might be time to consider a digital detox.

Case Studies and Examples

John's Weekend Digital Detox John, a marketing executive, struggled with constant connectivity and felt overwhelmed by the nonstop flow of emails and notifications. Deciding to take a weekend digital detox, John informed his colleagues and clients that he would be unavailable. He spent the weekend hiking, reading, and spending quality time with his family. By the end of the detox, John felt rejuvenated and more focused. He noticed that the break helped him reconnect with his family and significantly reduced his stress levels.

Sarah's Student Experience Sarah, a college student, found that her anxiety levels were increasing due to the pressure of constantly being online for both academic and social purposes. She decided to implement a digital detox during her spring break. Sarah replaced her screen time with yoga classes, cooking, and nature walks. By the end of the week, she felt more centered and less anxious. The detox not only improved her mental well-being but also helped her develop healthier habits, like setting boundaries for her screen time during school days.

Michael's Long-Term Strategy Michael, a software developer, realized that his productivity was suffering due to frequent digital distractions. He decided to implement a structured digital detox plan by setting tech-free times during his workday and creating a tech-free zone in his home office. Over the course of several months, Michael found that his focus and productivity improved significantly. He also experienced fewer headaches and less eye strain. Michael's long-term strategy involved regular digital detoxes, which helped him maintain a healthy balance between work and personal life.

Lila's Family Digital Detox Lila, a mother of two, noticed that her family spent most of their time on screens, leading to a lack of quality family interactions. She proposed a family digital detox weekend, where all family members would disconnect from their devices. Instead, they engaged in board games, outdoor activities, and cooking together. The experience brought the family closer, and they decided to make it a monthly tradition. The family digital detox not only improved their relationships but also promoted healthier screen habits for her children.

Conclusion

A digital detox can be a powerful tool for improving mental well-being and reconnecting with the physical world. By setting clear goals, establishing boundaries, finding alternatives, using tools to limit access, reflecting on the benefits, gradually reintroducing digital devices, and creating long-term habits, you can successfully implement a digital detox and experience its profound effects on your life. Embrace the opportunity to disconnect from digital distractions and reconnect with what truly matters.

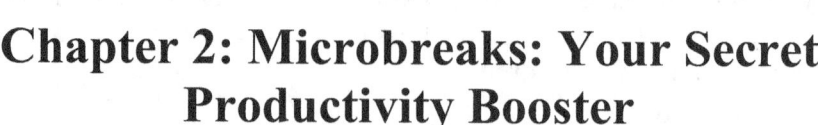

Chapter 2: Microbreaks: Your Secret Productivity Booster

T*he Whisper of the Breeze*

A disciple asked the wise sage, "How can I sustain my energy throughout the long hours of work?"

The sage smiled and said, "Look at the tall tree outside. It stands firm but sways with the breeze."

The disciple looked puzzled and asked, "What does the tree have to do with my work?"

The sage replied, "The tree does not fight the wind; it bends and moves with it. Every so often, it pauses, still and calm."

The disciple thought for a moment and then asked, "So, how should I work?"

The sage answered, "Work like the tree. Stand firm in your tasks, but let yourself sway with the gentle breeze of a microbreak. Pause, breathe, and move lightly. This way, you will remain strong and energized."

Inspired, the disciple began to take short, mindful breaks, finding renewed energy and focus in the rhythm of work and rest.

Introduction

In the fast-paced modern workplace, maintaining productivity and focus can be challenging. Microbreaks—short, frequent breaks taken throughout the day—can significantly enhance your productivity and well-being. This chapter delves into the science behind microbreaks and provides practical tips for incorporating them into your daily routine.

Understanding the Concept

Microbreaks involve taking brief pauses from work to rest and recharge. Unlike longer breaks, microbreaks are typically 1-5 minutes long and can be taken every 20-30 minutes. These breaks help prevent fatigue, reduce stress, and improve overall productivity.

Dr. Vincent Walsh from University College London explains that microbreaks help refresh the mind and body, preventing fatigue and maintaining productivity. Francesco Cirillo, the creator of the Pomodoro Technique, emphasizes the importance of regular breaks to sustain high levels of focus and efficiency.

The concept of microbreaks is rooted in cognitive psychology and occupational health. Our brains have a limited capacity for sustained attention, and prolonged periods of focus can lead to cognitive fatigue. Microbreaks provide an opportunity for mental recovery, allowing us to maintain a higher level of performance throughout the day. Additionally, microbreaks help alleviate physical discomfort associated with prolonged sitting and screen time.

Expert Insights and Research

A study published in the *Journal of Occupational Health Psychology* found that taking regular microbreaks can reduce stress and improve cognitive function. The Mayo Clinic also advocates for microbreaks as a means to reduce muscle strain and improve circulation, particularly for individuals who work in sedentary environments.

The American Optometric Association recommends the 20-20-20 rule to reduce eye strain: every 20 minutes, look at something 20 feet away for at least 20 seconds. This practice helps prevent digital eye strain and maintain eye health. Research from the National Institutes of Health suggests that personalized break schedules can optimize productivity and well-being.

A study by Dr. Emily Hunter and Dr. Cindy Wu at Baylor University found that employees who took microbreaks throughout the day reported higher levels of job satisfaction and reduced emotional exhaustion. Their research indicates that microbreaks allow employees to recover from work-related stress, leading to improved well-being and productivity.

Another study published in the *Journal of Applied Psychology* demonstrated that microbreaks could enhance work performance by preventing cognitive fatigue. Participants who took regular microbreaks performed better on tasks requiring sustained attention and showed fewer signs of mental exhaustion.

Practical Steps and Tips

1. Set a Timer Use a timer to remind yourself to take a break every 25-30 minutes. The Pomodoro Technique is a popular method that involves working for 25 minutes followed by a 5-minute break. This approach helps maintain focus while ensuring regular breaks. Using apps like Pomodone, Focus Booster, or Tomato Timer can help automate this process.

2. Move Around During your breaks, stand up, stretch, or take a short walk. Physical activity during breaks can help reduce muscle strain and improve circulation. The Mayo Clinic emphasizes the importance of movement to prevent the negative effects of prolonged sitting. Simple stretches like neck rolls, shoulder shrugs, and leg stretches can alleviate tension and promote blood flow.

3. Rest Your Eyes Follow the 20-20-20 rule to rest your eyes and reduce digital eye strain. This simple practice can help maintain eye health and prevent discomfort caused by prolonged screen time. Additionally, performing eye exercises like focusing on a distant object for a few seconds, then switching to a closer object, can help relax eye muscles.

4. Hydrate and Refresh Drink water or have a healthy snack during your breaks. Staying hydrated helps maintain cognitive function and energy levels. Proper hydration is essential for overall health and productivity. Including electrolytes in your hydration routine, such as those found in sports drinks or electrolyte tablets, can help maintain optimal hydration and energy levels.

5. Engage in Mindfulness Incorporate mindfulness practices into your microbreaks. Spend a few minutes focusing on your breath, practicing gratitude, or doing a quick meditation. Studies published in the *Journal of Occupational Health Psychology* show that mindfulness can enhance mental clarity and reduce stress. Simple mindfulness exercises include deep breathing, progressive muscle relaxation, and guided imagery.

6. Socialize Use some of your break time to connect with colleagues or friends. Social interaction can boost your mood and provide a mental reset. According to the *American Psychological Association*, socializing during breaks can improve overall job satisfaction and well-being. A quick chat with a colleague or a phone call to a friend can provide a positive distraction and enhance your social support network.

7. Reflect and Adjust Regularly review your break schedule and adjust it to fit your work pattern. Personalized break schedules can optimize productivity and well-being. Reflect on how different break intervals impact your focus and adjust accordingly. Keeping a journal to track your breaks and their effects on your productivity and mood can provide valuable insights for fine-tuning your routine.

Additional Tips for Effective Microbreaks

1. Create a Break-Friendly Environment Ensure your workspace is conducive to taking breaks. Arrange your desk to allow for easy movement and access to water and healthy snacks. Consider setting up a designated break area with comfortable seating and relaxing visuals, such as plants or artwork.

2. Practice Breathing Exercises Deep breathing exercises can help reduce stress and improve focus. Try the 4-7-8 technique: inhale for 4 seconds, hold your breath for 7 seconds, and exhale for 8 seconds. This exercise can calm your nervous system and provide a quick mental reset.

3. Use Technology to Your Advantage Leverage technology to help you take breaks. Apps like Stretchly, TimeOut, and EyeLeo can remind you to take breaks and provide suggestions for activities during your microbreaks. These tools can help you stay consistent and make the most of your break time.

4. Incorporate Physical Exercises Include simple physical exercises in your microbreaks to counteract the effects of prolonged sitting. Activities like desk push-ups, chair squats, and calf raises can improve circulation and prevent muscle stiffness. Incorporating short bursts of physical activity can also boost your energy levels and enhance cognitive function.

Do's and Don'ts of Microbreaks

Do's:

- **Do set a timer**: Use a timer to remind yourself to take breaks regularly.
- **Do move around**: Incorporate physical activity into your breaks.
- **Do follow the 20-20-20 rule**: Rest your eyes every 20 minutes.
- **Do hydrate and refresh**: Drink water and have healthy snacks.

- **Do engage in mindfulness**: Practice mindfulness techniques during breaks.
- **Do socialize**: Connect with colleagues or friends during breaks.
- **Do reflect and adjust**: Review and adjust your break schedule as needed.

Don'ts:

- **Don't skip breaks**: Avoid the temptation to work through breaks.
- **Don't stay sedentary**: Avoid remaining seated during breaks.
- **Don't use screens**: Refrain from using digital devices during breaks.
- **Don't ignore hydration**: Ensure you stay hydrated throughout the day.
- **Don't neglect mindfulness**: Incorporate mindfulness practices into your routine.
- **Don't isolate yourself**: Use breaks as an opportunity to socialize.
- **Don't stick to a rigid schedule**: Be flexible and adjust your break intervals based on your needs.

FAQ: Microbreaks

Q: How long should a microbreak last? A: Microbreaks typically last between 1-5 minutes. The key is to take them frequently, about every 20-30 minutes, to prevent fatigue and maintain focus.

Q: Can microbreaks really improve productivity? A: Yes, research shows that regular microbreaks can reduce stress, improve cognitive function, and enhance overall productivity. They help prevent burnout and maintain energy levels throughout the day.

Q: What are some good activities to do during a microbreak? A: Activities like stretching, taking a short walk, practicing deep breathing, drinking water, or chatting with a colleague are great options for a microbreak.

Q: How do I remember to take microbreaks? A: Use a timer or set reminders on your phone or computer. The Pomodoro Technique, which involves working for 25 minutes followed by a 5-minute break, is a popular method for incorporating microbreaks.

Q: Can microbreaks help with eye strain? A: Yes, following the 20-20-20 rule during microbreaks can help reduce digital eye strain. This rule involves looking at something 20 feet away for at least 20 seconds every 20 minutes.

Q: Can microbreaks include mindfulness practices? A: Absolutely. Incorporating mindfulness practices like deep breathing, meditation, or progressive muscle relaxation can enhance the restorative effects of microbreaks.

Q: How can I incorporate hydration into my microbreaks? A: Keep a water bottle at your desk and make it a habit to take a sip during each break. Adding electrolytes to your water can help maintain optimal hydration and energy levels.

Q: Are there specific physical exercises recommended for microbreaks? A: Simple exercises like desk push-ups, chair squats, calf raises, neck rolls, and shoulder shrugs are great options. These activities help improve circulation, reduce muscle stiffness, and boost energy levels.

Case Studies and Examples

Emily's Developer Routine Emily, a software developer, often experienced fatigue and eye strain from long hours in front of a screen. Implementing the 20-20-20 rule, she set up her computer to remind her to look away from the screen every 20 minutes. Additionally, Emily started taking short walks around her office building during her microbreaks. These changes led to a noticeable reduction in her eye strain and a boost in her overall productivity.

Mark's Project Management Strategy Mark, a project manager, found himself overwhelmed by back-to-back meetings and constant multitasking. He decided to implement the Pomodoro Technique, working for 25 minutes followed by a 5-minute break. During his breaks, Mark practiced deep breathing exercises and occasionally chatted with his team. This approach helped him manage his workload more effectively and maintain a higher level of focus throughout the day.

Sophia's Graphic Design Experience Sophia, a graphic designer, often worked on intense design projects that required long periods of concentration. She began incorporating microbreaks into her daily routine by using a timer to remind her to take breaks every 25 minutes. During her breaks, Sophia would stretch, drink water, and rest her eyes. These microbreaks helped her maintain her creativity and energy levels, leading to higher quality work and reduced fatigue.

John's Customer Service Approach John, a customer service representative, dealt with high volumes of customer inquiries and complaints. To manage the stress and maintain his performance, John started using microbreaks. He would take a short break after handling a few calls to stretch, breathe deeply, and clear his mind. These breaks allowed him to stay calm and focused, improving his overall job satisfaction and customer interactions.

Lisa's Teaching Routine Lisa, a high school teacher, found that her energy levels would often dip in the middle of the day. She started incorporating microbreaks into her teaching routine, using the breaks to stretch, drink water, and practice deep breathing. These short breaks helped Lisa maintain her energy and enthusiasm throughout the school day, positively impacting her teaching and interactions with students.

David's Remote Work Strategy David, a remote worker, struggled with maintaining focus and avoiding distractions at home. He implemented a structured microbreak schedule, taking a 5-minute break every 25 minutes. During his breaks, David would do quick exercises, drink water, and practice mindfulness. This routine helped him stay productive and focused, reducing the impact of home distractions on his work.

Conclusion

Microbreaks are a simple yet effective strategy for enhancing productivity and well-being. By setting a timer, moving around, resting your eyes, hydrating, engaging in mindfulness, socializing, and reflecting on your break schedule, you can incorporate microbreaks into your daily routine and experience their numerous benefits. Embrace the power of microbreaks to maintain energy, reduce stress, and boost productivity throughout your workday.

Chapter 3: Perfecting Screen Brightness for Health

T*he Screen's Glow*

A monk asked the master, "How can I find peace amidst the glow of the screen?"

The master replied, "When you stare into the screen, what do you see?"

The monk answered, "I see a thousand tasks and endless light."

The master said, "Close your eyes, and tell me what you see now."

The monk hesitated, then replied, "I see darkness, but I feel the presence of light."

The master nodded, "In the darkness, the mind finds rest. When the screen's glow becomes your sun, remember to close your eyes and embrace the night."

The monk, enlightened, adjusted his screen brightness and closed his eyes every twenty minutes, finding peace in the balance between light and dark.

Introduction

The digital age has brought with it numerous benefits, but it has also introduced new challenges, particularly when it comes to our visual health. One of the most overlooked aspects of digital wellness is screen brightness. This chapter explores the importance of optimal screen brightness for reducing eye strain and improving visual comfort, providing actionable tips for adjusting your screens for different environments.

Understanding Screen Brightness

Screen brightness refers to the amount of light emitted by a digital screen. While high brightness levels can make it easier to see content in bright environments, they can also cause eye strain and discomfort when used for extended periods. Conversely, low brightness levels can make it difficult to see content clearly, leading to increased eye strain as your eyes work harder to focus.

The Impact on Eye Health

Dr. Joshua Dunaief from the University of Pennsylvania explains that improper screen brightness can lead to digital eye strain, also known as computer vision syndrome. Symptoms include headaches, blurred vision, dry eyes, and neck and shoulder pain. According to the American Optometric Association, nearly 60% of Americans experience symptoms of digital eye strain, making it a widespread issue.

Blue Light and Sleep Disruption

Another factor to consider is the blue light emitted by digital screens. Blue light exposure, especially in the evening, can interfere with your sleep cycle by suppressing the production of melatonin, a hormone that regulates sleep. The National Sleep Foundation recommends reducing blue light exposure in the hours leading up to bedtime to improve sleep quality.

Understanding Optimal Screen Brightness

Optimal screen brightness involves adjusting your screen to match the ambient lighting of your environment. This helps reduce glare and prevent your eyes from working too hard to adjust to the screen's light. Dr. Jeff Anshel from the Ocular Nutrition Society emphasizes that optimal screen brightness can significantly reduce the risk of digital eye strain and improve overall visual comfort.

Expert Insights and Research

Research published in the *Journal of Ophthalmology* highlights the importance of adjusting screen brightness to match the ambient lighting in your environment. The study found that individuals who adjusted their screen brightness based on surrounding light conditions experienced fewer symptoms of eye strain and discomfort.

Dr. Lisa Ostrin from the University of Houston has conducted research on the effects of screen brightness and blue light exposure on eye health. Her studies suggest that reducing screen brightness and using blue light filters can help prevent digital eye strain and improve sleep quality. Additionally, Dr. Ostrin recommends regular eye exams to monitor and address any vision issues related to screen use.

The Vision Council reports that using blue light filters can reduce the negative effects of blue light exposure, improving sleep quality and reducing eye strain. According to a report by the American Academy of Ophthalmology, adjusting screen settings to reduce glare and match ambient lighting can enhance visual comfort and prevent eye strain.

Practical Steps and Tips

1. Use Built-In Blue Light Filters Most modern devices have built-in blue light filters. For example, Apple devices offer Night Shift, while Android devices have Blue Light Filter. These settings reduce blue light exposure, making it easier on your eyes and improving sleep quality. Dr. Lisa Ostrin from the University of Houston recommends using these filters, especially in the evening.

2. Adjust Brightness to Ambient Light Ensure your screen brightness matches the ambient lighting in your environment. The American Academy of Ophthalmology suggests using automatic brightness adjustment features available on most devices. These features adjust the screen brightness based on the surrounding light, reducing glare and preventing eye strain.

3. Use Anti-Glare Screens Anti-glare screens can minimize reflections and glare from your monitor. Dr. Jeff Anshel advocates for the use of anti-glare screens to enhance visual comfort, especially in brightly lit environments. Anti-glare screens are available as add-ons for most devices and can significantly improve your viewing experience.

4. Maintain an Ergonomic Setup Position your monitor at eye level, about 20-30 inches away from your face. The American Optometric Association recommends this setup to prevent neck and eye strain. Additionally, using a document holder to place reading materials at the same height as your monitor can reduce the need for frequent eye and neck movements.

5. Take Regular Breaks Follow the 20-20-20 rule: every 20 minutes, look at something 20 feet away for at least 20 seconds. This practice helps reduce digital eye strain and maintain eye health. Regular breaks allow your eyes to rest and refocus, preventing fatigue and discomfort.

6. Blink More Often When staring at a screen, people tend to blink less frequently, leading to dry eyes. Make a conscious effort to blink more often to keep your eyes moist. The American Academy of Ophthalmology suggests using artificial tears if needed to alleviate dryness.

7. Adjust Text Size and Contrast Increasing text size and adjusting contrast settings can help reduce eye strain. Larger text is easier to read, and proper contrast ensures that text stands out against the background. Most devices and applications have settings that allow you to customize these aspects for better visual comfort.

Additional Tips for Maintaining Visual Health

1. Regular Eye Exams Schedule regular eye exams to monitor and address any vision issues related to screen use. Dr. Joshua Dunaief emphasizes the importance of routine check-ups to ensure your eyes are healthy and to catch any problems early.

2. Proper Lighting Ensure your workspace is well-lit to reduce the strain on your eyes. Avoid working in dim lighting or under harsh fluorescent lights. Natural light is ideal, but if that's not possible, use soft, indirect lighting to minimize glare and shadows.

3. Blue Light Glasses Consider using blue light-blocking glasses if you spend a lot of time in front of screens. These glasses can help filter out blue light and reduce eye strain. Studies published in the *Journal of Adolescent Health* have shown that blue light-blocking glasses can improve sleep quality and reduce symptoms of digital eye strain.

4. Ergonomic Accessories Use ergonomic accessories like monitor stands, adjustable chairs, and footrests to create a comfortable and healthy workspace. These tools can help you maintain proper posture and reduce the risk of developing musculoskeletal problems.

5. Hydration Staying hydrated is essential for maintaining eye health. Drink plenty of water throughout the day to keep your eyes moist and reduce the risk of dryness and irritation.

Do's and Don'ts of Screen Brightness

Do's:

- **Do use built-in blue light filters**: Enable blue light filters on your devices, especially in the evening.

- **Do adjust brightness to ambient light**: Match your screen brightness to the surrounding lighting conditions.

- **Do use anti-glare screens**: Invest in anti-glare screens to reduce reflections and glare.

- **Do maintain an ergonomic setup**: Position your monitor at eye level and use ergonomic accessories.

- **Do take regular breaks**: Follow the 20-20-20 rule to rest your eyes and prevent strain.

- **Do blink often**: Make a conscious effort to blink more frequently to keep your eyes moist.

- **Do adjust text size and contrast**: Customize text size and contrast settings for better visual comfort.

- **Do have regular eye exams**: Schedule routine eye exams to monitor and address vision issues.

Don'ts:

- **Don't use high brightness levels for extended periods**: Avoid using high screen brightness in low-light environments.

- **Don't ignore eye discomfort**: Address any symptoms of eye strain or discomfort promptly.

- **Don't work in dim lighting**: Ensure your workspace is well-lit to reduce eye strain.

- **Don't forget to take breaks**: Regular breaks are essential for maintaining eye health.

- **Don't neglect hydration**: Stay hydrated to keep your eyes moist and healthy.

- **Don't use screens before bed**: Minimize screen use in the hours leading up to bedtime to improve sleep quality.

- **Don't overlook ergonomic setups**: Proper ergonomics are crucial for reducing eye and musculoskeletal strain.

FAQ: Screen Brightness

Q: How do I know if my screen brightness is too high or too low? A: If your screen is causing glare or discomfort, it may be too bright. Conversely, if you have to strain to see the content, it may be too dim. Adjust the brightness to a comfortable level that matches the ambient lighting in your environment.

Q: Can blue light filters really improve sleep quality? A: Yes, blue light filters can help reduce the negative impact of blue light on your sleep cycle. Blue light exposure in the evening can suppress melatonin production, making it harder to fall asleep. Using blue light filters can improve sleep quality.

Q: What are the benefits of using anti-glare screens? A: Anti-glare screens reduce reflections and glare from your monitor, making it easier to see the content and reducing eye strain. They are particularly useful in brightly lit environments.

Q: How often should I take breaks to rest my eyes? A: Follow the 20-20-20 rule: every 20 minutes, look at something 20 feet away for at least 20 seconds. This helps reduce digital eye strain and maintain eye health.

Q: Are blue light-blocking glasses effective? A: Studies have shown that blue light-blocking glasses can improve sleep quality and reduce symptoms of digital eye strain. They can be a useful tool for individuals who spend a lot of time in front of screens.

Q: How can I reduce eye strain while reading on a screen? A: Increase the text size, adjust the contrast, and ensure your screen brightness matches the ambient light. Taking regular breaks and following the 20-20-20 rule can also help reduce eye strain.

Case Studies and Examples

Anne's Improved Visual Comfort Anne, a graphic designer, frequently experienced headaches and eye strain after long hours of work. She decided to adjust her screen brightness based on the ambient light in her workspace and started using a blue light filter in the evenings. Additionally, Anne incorporated the 20-20-20 rule into her routine. Within a few weeks, she noticed a significant reduction in her symptoms and an improvement in her overall visual comfort.

Michael's Experience with Anti-Glare Screens Michael, a software engineer, worked in a brightly lit office with large windows. The glare on his monitor made it difficult to see clearly, causing eye strain and discomfort. Michael installed an anti-glare screen on his monitor and adjusted the screen brightness to match the ambient light. These changes greatly improved his visual comfort and reduced his eye strain, allowing him to work more efficiently.

Rachel's Ergonomic Workspace Rachel, a writer, often worked late into the night on her laptop. She noticed that her sleep quality was deteriorating, and she felt constantly fatigued. Rachel began using her laptop's built-in blue light filter in the evenings and adjusted her screen brightness to a lower setting. She also made ergonomic adjustments to her workspace, including using a monitor stand and an adjustable chair. These changes not only reduced her eye strain but also improved her sleep quality and overall well-being.

Joe's Commitment to Regular Eye Exams Joe, an accountant, spent most of his day working on spreadsheets. He experienced frequent dry eyes and blurry vision. Joe decided to schedule regular eye exams to monitor his eye health. His optometrist recommended using artificial tears and adjusting his screen brightness to match the ambient light. Joe also started using blue light-blocking glasses. These steps helped alleviate his symptoms and maintained his visual health.

Conclusion

Optimizing screen brightness is a crucial aspect of digital wellness that can significantly reduce eye strain and improve visual comfort. By using built-in blue light filters, adjusting brightness to ambient light, using anti-glare screens, maintaining an ergonomic setup, taking regular breaks, blinking more often, and adjusting text size and contrast, you can protect your eyes and enhance your overall digital experience. Implement these strategies to maintain eye health and improve your productivity in the digital age.

Chapter 4: Radical Digital Minimalism

The Empty Bowl

A young monk approached the master and asked, "How can I find tranquility amidst the chaos of my digital life?"

The master handed the monk an empty bowl and said, "Fill this bowl with water."

The monk filled the bowl to the brim, and the master then added a stone. The water overflowed and spilled onto the ground.

The master asked, "What do you see?"

The monk replied, "The bowl is too full; it cannot hold more without losing some."

The master nodded, "Now, empty the bowl and fill it only halfway."

The monk did as instructed. The master added the stone again, and this time, the water adjusted but did not overflow.

The master said, "Your digital life is like this bowl. When filled to the brim with unnecessary things, even a small addition causes overflow and chaos. Keep it half full, holding only what is essential, and you will find tranquility."

The monk understood and began practicing digital minimalism, finding peace in a life less cluttered.

Introduction

In an age where we are constantly bombarded with digital information, the concept of digital minimalism offers a refreshing approach to managing our digital lives. Digital minimalism is about focusing on what truly matters and eliminating the excess. This chapter explores the principles of digital minimalism and provides practical strategies to help you declutter your digital life and enhance your overall well-being.

Understanding Digital Minimalism

Digital minimalism involves intentionally reducing the time and effort spent on digital devices and platforms to focus on meaningful and valuable activities. It is not about completely eliminating technology but about using it in a way that aligns with your values and goals.

Cal Newport, author of *Digital Minimalism: Choosing a Focused Life in a Noisy World*, describes digital minimalism as a philosophy that helps individuals regain control over their digital consumption. Newport emphasizes the importance of intentional use of technology, advocating for a more deliberate and mindful approach to digital engagement.

Expert Insights and Research

Marie Kondo, author of *The Life-Changing Magic of Tidying Up*, applies her principles of decluttering to the digital realm, suggesting that we keep only those digital tools and platforms that "spark joy." Kondo's method involves a thorough examination of our digital possessions and a conscious decision to retain only those that add value to our lives.

Research by the *Pew Research Center* highlights that excessive use of digital devices can lead to increased stress, anxiety, and decreased productivity. The study found that individuals who practiced digital minimalism reported higher levels of satisfaction and well-being.

A study published in the *Journal of Behavioral Addictions* found that reducing screen time and limiting digital distractions can lead to significant improvements in mental health and cognitive function. Participants who adopted digital minimalism strategies experienced lower levels of anxiety and improved focus and productivity.

Practical Steps and Tips

1. Conduct a Digital Declutter Begin by evaluating your digital devices, apps, and platforms. Identify those that are essential and those that can be eliminated. Marie Kondo's method of asking whether an item "sparks joy" can be applied to your digital possessions. Remove unnecessary apps, unsubscribe from unneeded newsletters, and delete old files and emails.

2. Set Clear Intentions Define your goals and priorities when it comes to digital usage. Determine what is most important to you and align your digital activities with these values. Cal Newport suggests creating a "digital declutter" plan, where you take a 30-day break from optional technologies and reintroduce only those that add significant value to your life.

3. Limit Social Media Use Social media can be a major source of digital clutter. Consider limiting your use of social media platforms to specific times of the day or setting a daily time limit. Use tools like Screen Time on iOS or Digital Wellbeing on Android to monitor and control your usage.

4. Embrace Single-Tasking Focus on one task at a time instead of multitasking. Multitasking can lead to decreased productivity and increased stress. By concentrating on a single task, you can improve your efficiency and reduce cognitive overload.

5. Create Tech-Free Zones Designate areas in your home where digital devices are not allowed. This could include the dining room, bedroom, or living room. Creating tech-free zones helps reinforce boundaries and encourages more meaningful offline interactions.

6. Schedule Digital Downtime Set aside specific times during the day for digital downtime. This could be in the evenings before bed, during meals, or on weekends. Use this time to engage in offline activities that you enjoy, such as reading, exercising, or spending time with loved ones.

7. Practice Mindful Technology Use Be intentional about how you use technology. Before reaching for your phone or opening an app, ask yourself whether it aligns with your goals and values. Mindful technology use involves being aware of your habits and making conscious choices about your digital consumption.

Additional Tips for Digital Minimalism

1. Use Productivity Tools Utilize productivity tools like task managers, calendar apps, and focus apps to streamline your digital tasks. Tools like Todoist, Trello, and Focus@Will can help you stay organized and focused on your priorities.

2. Set Boundaries with Notifications Turn off non-essential notifications to reduce distractions. Customize your notification settings to ensure that only important alerts come through. This can help minimize interruptions and maintain your focus.

3. Digital Detox Days Incorporate regular digital detox days into your schedule. These are days when you completely disconnect from digital devices and engage in offline activities. Digital detox days can provide a much-needed break from screens and help reset your relationship with technology.

4. Limit Information Consumption Be selective about the information you consume online. Subscribe only to newsletters, podcasts, and channels that provide value and align with your interests. Avoid mindlessly scrolling through news feeds and focus on quality content.

5. Engage in Analog Activities Incorporate more analog activities into your routine. This could include journaling, drawing, playing a musical instrument, or spending time in nature. Analog activities can provide a break from screens and promote creativity and relaxation.

Do's and Don'ts of Digital Minimalism
Do's:

- **Do conduct a digital declutter**: Evaluate and eliminate unnecessary digital possessions.

- **Do set clear intentions**: Align your digital activities with your values and goals.

- **Do limit social media use**: Monitor and control your social media usage.

- **Do embrace single-tasking**: Focus on one task at a time for improved productivity.

- **Do create tech-free zones**: Designate areas in your home where digital devices are not allowed.

- **Do schedule digital downtime**: Set aside specific times for engaging in offline activities.

- **Do practice mindful technology use**: Make conscious choices about your digital consumption.

- **Do use productivity tools**: Utilize tools to streamline your digital tasks.

- **Do set boundaries with notifications**: Customize notification settings to reduce distractions.

- **Do incorporate digital detox days**: Regularly disconnect from digital devices.

Don'ts:

- **Don't ignore digital clutter**: Address and eliminate unnecessary digital possessions.

- **Don't multitask**: Avoid multitasking as it can decrease productivity and increase stress.

- **Don't let social media control you**: Set limits on your social media usage.

- **Don't neglect analog activities**: Engage in offline activities that promote creativity and relaxation.

- **Don't allow notifications to disrupt you**: Turn off non-essential notifications to maintain focus.

- **Don't consume information mindlessly**: Be selective about the information you consume online.

- **Don't forget to take breaks**: Incorporate regular breaks from digital devices to reset and recharge.

FAQ: Digital Minimalism

Q: What is digital minimalism? A: Digital minimalism is the intentional reduction of digital devices and platforms to focus on meaningful and valuable activities. It involves using technology in a way that aligns with your values and goals.

Q: How do I start practicing digital minimalism? A: Begin by conducting a digital declutter, setting clear intentions for your digital usage, and limiting social media use. Create tech-free zones, schedule digital downtime, and practice mindful technology use.

Q: Can digital minimalism improve mental health? A: Yes, research shows that digital minimalism can lead to significant improvements in mental health, including reduced stress, anxiety, and increased focus and productivity.

Q: How can I limit my social media use? A: Set specific times of the day for social media use, use tools like Screen Time or Digital Wellbeing to monitor and control usage, and consider deleting or limiting access to non-essential social media apps.

Q: What are tech-free zones? A: Tech-free zones are designated areas in your home where digital devices are not allowed. These areas encourage more meaningful offline interactions and help reinforce boundaries with technology.

Q: How often should I take digital detox days? A: The frequency of digital detox days depends on your personal preferences and needs. Some people may benefit from a digital detox day once a week, while others may prefer once a month. Experiment to find what works best for you.

Case Studies and Examples

Emily's Digital Declutter Emily, a marketing professional, felt overwhelmed by the constant influx of emails, social media notifications, and digital distractions. She decided to conduct a digital declutter by deleting unnecessary apps, unsubscribing from unneeded newsletters, and organizing her files. Emily also set clear intentions for her digital usage, focusing on professional development and meaningful connections. As a result, Emily experienced reduced stress and increased productivity.

Mark's Mindful Technology Use Mark, a teacher, realized that he was spending too much time on his phone, often mindlessly scrolling through social media. He decided to practice mindful technology use by setting specific goals for his digital activities and limiting his social media usage to 30 minutes per day. Mark also created tech-free zones in his home and scheduled digital downtime in the evenings. These changes helped Mark feel more present and engaged in his personal and professional life.

Annie's Single-Tasking Approach Annie, a software developer, often found herself multitasking and feeling scattered. She decided to embrace single-tasking by focusing on one task at a time and using productivity tools to stay organized. Annie also limited her social media use and created tech-free zones in her home. As a result, Annie experienced increased focus and efficiency, completing tasks more effectively and with less stress.

John's Digital Detox Days John, a graphic designer, felt that he was constantly connected to his devices, leading to burnout and decreased creativity. He decided to incorporate regular digital detox days into his schedule, where he would completely disconnect from digital devices and engage in offline activities like hiking, reading, and painting. These detox days helped John recharge and regain his creativity, improving his overall well-being.

Jane's Balanced Digital Life Jane, a college student, struggled with balancing her academic responsibilities and digital distractions. She decided to adopt digital minimalism by conducting a digital declutter, setting clear intentions for her digital usage, and limiting social media use. Jane also practiced mindful technology use, created tech-free zones, and scheduled digital downtime. These changes helped Jane achieve a balanced digital life, reducing stress and improving her focus and academic performance.

Conclusion

Radical digital minimalism offers a powerful approach to managing your digital life by focusing on what truly matters and eliminating the excess. By conducting a digital declutter, setting clear intentions, limiting social media use, embracing single-tasking, creating tech-free zones, scheduling digital downtime, and practicing mindful technology use, you can declutter your digital life and enhance your overall well-being. Embrace the principles of digital minimalism to regain control over your digital consumption and create a more intentional and meaningful relationship with technology.

Chapter 5: Building the Ultimate Distraction-Free Workspace

T*he Silent Garden*

A disciple, seeking focus, approached the master and asked, "How can I create a space free of distractions to concentrate on my work?"

The master led the disciple to a garden filled with overgrown weeds, noisy birds, and scattered tools. "Work here," the master instructed.

The disciple tried but found the noise and chaos overwhelming. Frustrated, he returned to the master, who then took him to a different garden. This garden was serene, with neatly trimmed plants, flowing water, and a quiet atmosphere.

The master asked, "Which garden helps you focus?"

The disciple replied, "The quiet, organized garden. Here, I can concentrate without distraction."

The master nodded, "Your workspace is like a garden. Clear the weeds of clutter, trim the noise of interruptions, and arrange your tools with care. Create a space where your mind can flow like water, and you will find focus."

The disciple understood and began transforming his workspace into a sanctuary of calm and order, finding the focus and productivity he sought.

Introduction

IN TODAY'S FAST-PACED and hyper-connected world, maintaining focus and productivity can be challenging. A well-designed, distraction-free workspace can significantly enhance your ability to concentrate and get work done efficiently. This chapter explores the principles of creating an optimal workspace that minimizes distractions and maximizes productivity.

Understanding the Concept

A DISTRACTION-FREE workspace is an environment specifically designed to eliminate interruptions and foster concentration. This involves carefully organizing physical and digital elements to create a conducive atmosphere for focused work. Dr. Gloria Mark, a professor at the University of California, Irvine, explains that minimizing distractions in your workspace can significantly enhance your productivity and overall well-being.

Expert Insights and Research

RESEARCH PUBLISHED in the *Journal of Environmental Psychology* highlights the importance of a well-organized and clutter-free workspace. The study found that individuals working in a clean and organized environment experienced lower levels of stress and higher levels of productivity.

Dr. Alan Hedge, a professor of ergonomics at Cornell University, emphasizes the importance of ergonomic design in creating a distraction-free workspace. Proper ergonomic setups can prevent physical discomfort and improve overall work performance. Additionally, research from the *Journal of Occupational Health Psychology* suggests that personalizing your workspace can enhance job satisfaction and reduce stress.

A study by the *Journal of the Acoustical Society of America* found that ambient noise and interruptions can significantly impact cognitive performance. The study suggests using sound masking techniques and noise-canceling devices to reduce auditory distractions.

Practical Steps and Tips

1. DECLUTTER YOUR WORKSPACE Start by removing unnecessary items from your workspace. A cluttered desk can be visually distracting and make it harder to focus. Keep only essential items on your desk and store the rest in drawers or shelves. Marie

Kondo's principles of tidying up can be applied here—keep only those items that "spark joy" and are necessary for your work.

2. Optimize Ergonomics Ensure your workspace is ergonomically designed to prevent physical discomfort and strain. Dr. Alan Hedge recommends the following ergonomic guidelines:

- **Chair**: Use an adjustable chair that supports your lower back. Ensure your feet are flat on the floor, and your knees are at a 90-degree angle.

- **Desk**: Position your desk at a height where your elbows are at a 90-degree angle when typing.

- **Monitor**: Place your monitor at eye level, about 20-30 inches away from your face, to reduce neck strain.

3. Minimize Digital Distractions Limit digital interruptions by turning off non-essential notifications on your devices. Use tools like Freedom, StayFocusd, or Focus@Will to block distracting websites and apps during work hours. Organize your digital workspace by creating folders for different types of files and keeping your desktop clutter-free.

4. Create a Dedicated Work Zone Designate a specific area in your home or office for work-related activities. This helps create a mental boundary between work and personal life, making it easier to focus when you're in your designated work zone. Ensure this area is quiet and free from distractions.

5. Use Sound Masking Techniques Ambient noise can be a significant distraction. Use sound masking techniques such as white noise machines, noise-canceling headphones, or background music to reduce auditory distractions. Studies from the *Journal of the Acoustical Society of America* suggest that these techniques can improve focus and productivity.

6. Personalize Your Workspace Adding personal touches to your workspace can make it more inviting and comfortable. Personal items like family photos, plants, or artwork can enhance your mood and reduce stress. A study from the *Journal of Occupational Health Psychology* found that personalized workspaces contribute to higher job satisfaction and well-being.

7. Maintain a Clean and Organized Space Regularly clean and organize your workspace to maintain a distraction-free environment. A tidy workspace can reduce stress and create a more pleasant work atmosphere. Set aside time each week to declutter and reorganize your desk and digital files.

Additional Tips for a Distraction-Free Workspace

1. INCORPORATE NATURAL Elements Bringing elements of nature into your workspace can enhance your mood and productivity. Plants, natural light, and nature-themed artwork can create a calming environment. A study published in the *Journal of Environmental Psychology* found that incorporating natural elements into the workspace can reduce stress and improve cognitive function.

2. Use Visual Aids Visual aids like whiteboards, corkboards, or sticky notes can help you stay organized and focused. Use these tools to keep track of tasks, deadlines, and important information. Visual aids can provide a quick reference and help you stay on track with your work.

3. Establish a Routine Creating a consistent work routine can help you stay focused and productive. Set specific work hours, take regular breaks, and establish a start and end time for your workday. Consistency can help create a sense of structure and reduce distractions.

4. Limit Multitasking Focus on one task at a time to improve your efficiency and reduce cognitive overload. Multitasking can lead to decreased productivity and increased stress. Prioritize your tasks and work on them sequentially to maintain focus.

5. Invest in Quality Equipment Using high-quality equipment can enhance your work experience and reduce distractions. Invest in a comfortable chair, a reliable computer, and any other tools you need for your work. Quality equipment can improve your efficiency and overall job satisfaction.

Do's and Don'ts of a Distraction-Free Workspace

DO'S:

- **Do declutter regularly**: Keep your workspace clean and organized.

- **Do optimize ergonomics**: Ensure your workspace is ergonomically designed to prevent discomfort.

- **Do minimize digital distractions**: Turn off non-essential notifications and use focus tools.

- **Do create a dedicated work zone**: Designate a specific area for work-related activities.

- **Do use sound masking techniques**: Reduce auditory distractions with white noise machines or noise-canceling headphones.

- **Do personalize your workspace**: Add personal touches to make your workspace more inviting.

- **Do incorporate natural elements**: Use plants and natural light to create a calming environment.

- **Do use visual aids**: Keep track of tasks and important information with visual aids.

- **Do establish a routine**: Create a consistent work routine to maintain focus.

- **Do invest in quality equipment**: Use reliable and comfortable equipment to enhance your work experience.

Don'ts:

- **Don't let clutter accumulate**: Regularly clean and organize your workspace.

- **Don't ignore ergonomics**: Proper ergonomics are essential for preventing discomfort.

- **Don't multitask**: Focus on one task at a time to improve efficiency.

- **Don't allow digital distractions**: Turn off notifications and use focus tools.

- **Don't work in a noisy environment**: Use sound masking techniques to reduce auditory distractions.

- **Don't neglect personalization**: Add personal touches to make your workspace more inviting.

- **Don't overlook natural elements**: Incorporate plants and natural light into your workspace.

- **Don't forget visual aids**: Use whiteboards, corkboards, or sticky notes to stay organized.

- **Don't skip breaks**: Take regular breaks to maintain focus and prevent burnout.

- **Don't use poor-quality equipment**: Invest in reliable and comfortable tools for your work.

FAQ: Distraction-Free Workspace

Q: HOW DO I START CREATING a distraction-free workspace? A: Begin by decluttering your workspace, optimizing ergonomics, and minimizing digital distractions. Create a dedicated work zone, use sound masking techniques, and personalize your workspace.

Q: What are some tips for minimizing digital distractions? A: Turn off non-essential notifications, use tools like Freedom or StayFocusd to block distracting websites, and organize your digital workspace by creating folders for different types of files.

Q: How can I incorporate natural elements into my workspace? A: Add plants, use natural light, and incorporate nature-themed artwork. These elements can create a calming environment and improve your mood and productivity.

Q: What are sound masking techniques? A: Sound masking techniques include using white noise machines, noise-canceling headphones, or background music to reduce auditory distractions and improve focus.

Q: Why is ergonomics important in a workspace? A: Proper ergonomics prevent physical discomfort and strain, improving overall work performance and well-being. Ensure your chair, desk, and monitor are positioned correctly to support good posture.

Q: How often should I declutter my workspace? A: Regularly clean and organize your workspace to maintain a distraction-free environment. Set aside time each week to declutter and reorganize your desk and digital files.

Q: Can personalizing my workspace improve productivity? A: Yes, personalizing your workspace with items like family photos, plants, or artwork can enhance your mood, reduce stress, and improve job satisfaction.

Q: How can I establish a consistent work routine? A: Set specific work hours, take regular breaks, and establish a start and end time for your workday. Consistency can create a sense of structure and reduce distractions.

Q: What should I consider when investing in quality equipment? A: Invest in a comfortable chair, a reliable computer, and any other tools you need for your work. Quality equipment can improve your efficiency and overall job satisfaction.

Case Studies and Examples

MARGOT'S PRODUCTIVE Workspace Margot, a graphic designer, often felt overwhelmed by the clutter on her desk. She decided to declutter her workspace by removing unnecessary items and organizing her files. Margo also invested in an ergonomic chair and adjusted her monitor to eye level. Additionally, she used noise-canceling headphones to reduce auditory distractions. These changes significantly improved her focus and productivity, allowing her to complete her projects more efficiently.

John's Personalized Work Zone John, a software developer, worked from home and struggled to maintain focus with the various distractions around him. He created a dedicated work zone in his home office and personalized it with family photos and plants. John also used a white noise machine to mask background noise and set specific work hours to establish a routine. These adjustments helped John stay focused and productive throughout the day.

Rachel's Ergonomic Setup Rachel, a writer, often experienced neck and back pain from sitting at her desk for long periods. She decided to optimize her workspace ergonomics by using an adjustable chair and positioning her monitor at eye level. Rachel also incorporated regular breaks into her routine and used a standing desk converter to alternate between sitting and standing. These changes alleviated her discomfort and improved her overall well-being and productivity.

Mark's Clutter-Free Desk Mark, a project manager, found that his cluttered desk was a significant source of distraction. He decided to conduct a thorough declutter, removing unnecessary items and organizing his documents. Mark also used visual aids like a whiteboard to keep track of tasks and deadlines. These changes helped Mark create a more organized and focused work environment, enhancing his efficiency and reducing stress.

Emily's Sound Masking Techniques Emily, a customer service representative, worked in a noisy office environment that made it difficult to concentrate. She invested in noise-canceling headphones and used background music to mask distracting sounds. Emily also personalized her workspace with calming nature-themed artwork and plants. These adjustments helped Emily improve her focus and productivity, allowing her to handle customer inquiries more effectively.

Conclusion

CREATING A DISTRACTION-free workspace is essential for maintaining focus and productivity in today's hyper-connected world. By decluttering your workspace, optimizing ergonomics, minimizing digital distractions, creating a dedicated work zone, using sound masking techniques, personalizing your workspace, and maintaining a clean and organized environment, you can enhance your ability to concentrate and get work done efficiently. Implement these strategies to create an optimal workspace that supports your productivity and well-being.

Chapter 6: Blue Light Filters: Why You Need Them

The Gentle Sunset

A student asked the sage, "Why do my eyes feel tired and my sleep restless after staring at screens all day?"

The sage took the student to a hilltop at dusk and said, "Watch the sunset."

The student watched as the bright day slowly softened into the gentle hues of evening, feeling a sense of calm wash over them.

The sage then asked, "What do you feel now?"

The student replied, "Peaceful and ready for rest."

The sage nodded and said, "The light of the day is like the blue light from your screens, intense and unyielding. The sunset is like the blue light filter, softening the light and preparing your mind for rest. Just as the sunset transitions you into night, let blue light filters ease your eyes and mind."

The student understood and began using blue light filters, finding their eyes less strained and their sleep more restful.

Introduction

IN OUR DIGITAL AGE, screens are an integral part of our daily lives. From smartphones to computers to televisions, we are constantly exposed to screens emitting blue light. While blue light is a natural part of sunlight and necessary for our well-being during the day, excessive exposure, especially during the evening, can have adverse effects on our health. This chapter explores the importance of blue light filters, their benefits, and practical tips for integrating them into your daily routine.

Understanding Blue Light

BLUE LIGHT IS A HIGH-energy visible (HEV) light with short wavelengths, ranging from 380 to 500 nanometers. It is part of the visible light spectrum and has both beneficial and harmful effects. During daylight hours, blue light helps regulate our circadian rhythms, boost alertness, and improve cognitive function. However, excessive exposure, especially during nighttime, can disrupt sleep patterns and lead to digital eye strain.

Impact on Sleep

DR. CHARLES CZEISLER from Harvard Medical School has conducted extensive research on the effects of blue light on sleep. His studies show that exposure to blue light in the evening suppresses the production of melatonin, a hormone that regulates sleep. This can lead to difficulties in falling asleep and poor sleep quality.

Digital Eye Strain

DR. LISA OSTRIN FROM the University of Houston explains that blue light exposure can contribute to digital eye strain, characterized by symptoms such as dry eyes, headaches, blurred vision, and discomfort. The American Optometric Association highlights that digital eye strain affects nearly 60% of Americans who use digital devices for extended periods.

Expert Insights and Research

RESEARCH PUBLISHED in the *Journal of Circadian Rhythms* indicates that reducing blue light exposure in the evening can significantly improve sleep quality and overall health. The study found that individuals who used blue light filters or avoided screens before bedtime experienced better sleep and felt more rested in the morning.

    The Vision Council reports that blue light exposure can contribute to long-term eye health issues, including macular degeneration. The council recommends using blue light filters to mitigate these risks. Additionally, Dr. Joshua Dunaief, an ophthalmologist at the University of Pennsylvania, emphasizes the importance of protecting our eyes from excessive blue light to maintain long-term visual health.

Practical Steps and Tips

1. USE BUILT-IN BLUE Light Filters Most modern devices have built-in blue light filters. For example, Apple devices offer Night Shift, which adjusts the display to warmer tones in the evening. Android devices have a similar feature called Blue Light Filter. Enabling these settings can help reduce blue light exposure and minimize its impact on your sleep and eye health.

2. Invest in Blue Light Blocking Glasses Blue light blocking glasses are designed to filter out blue light from screens. These glasses can be particularly useful for individuals who spend long hours in front of screens, especially during the evening. Dr. Lisa Ostrin recommends using these glasses to reduce digital eye strain and improve sleep quality.

3. Adjust Screen Brightness and Contrast Lowering the brightness and adjusting the contrast of your screens can help reduce the amount of blue light emitted. The American Academy of Ophthalmology suggests setting your screen brightness to match the ambient light in your environment. This not only reduces blue light exposure but also minimizes eye strain.

4. Take Regular Breaks Follow the 20-20-20 rule: every 20 minutes, look at something 20 feet away for at least 20 seconds. This practice helps reduce digital eye strain and gives your eyes a break from blue light exposure. Additionally, taking regular breaks can help maintain your focus and productivity throughout the day.

5. Limit Screen Time Before Bed Try to avoid using screens at least an hour before bedtime. Engaging in activities like reading a book, taking a warm bath, or practicing relaxation techniques can help prepare your body for sleep. Dr. Charles Czeisler's research emphasizes the importance of creating a screen-free bedtime routine to improve sleep quality.

6. Use Blue Light Filter Apps Several apps are available that can filter blue light from your screens. Apps like f.lux, Twilight, and Iris can adjust the color temperature of your screens based on the time of day. These apps are particularly useful for devices that do not have built-in blue light filters.

7. Optimize Lighting in Your Environment Consider using dim, warm-colored lights in your home during the evening. This can help reduce blue light exposure and create a more relaxing atmosphere. The Vision Council recommends using LED bulbs with lower color temperatures to minimize blue light emissions.

Additional Tips for Managing Blue Light Exposure

1. POSITION YOUR SCREENS Correctly Ensure that your screens are positioned at eye level and at an appropriate distance to reduce glare and minimize blue light exposure. The American Optometric Association suggests positioning your screen about 20-30 inches away from your eyes and slightly below eye level.

2. Use Anti-Reflective Screen Protectors Anti-reflective screen protectors can help reduce glare and blue light exposure. These protectors are available for most devices and can enhance visual comfort while using screens.

3. Incorporate Mindfulness Practices Incorporate mindfulness practices such as meditation, deep breathing, or yoga into your evening routine to help reduce stress and prepare for sleep. These practices can complement your efforts to minimize blue light exposure and improve sleep quality.

4. Monitor Your Screen Time Be mindful of your overall screen time and set limits to avoid excessive exposure. Use features like Screen Time on iOS or Digital Wellbeing on Android to track and manage your screen usage. Setting daily limits can help you maintain a healthy balance between screen time and offline activities.

Do's and Don'ts of Blue Light Management

DO'S:

- **Do use built-in blue light filters**: Enable blue light filters on your devices, especially in the evening.

- **Do invest in blue light blocking glasses**: Use these glasses to reduce digital eye strain and improve sleep quality.

- **Do adjust screen brightness and contrast**: Lower brightness and adjust contrast to match ambient light.

- **Do take regular breaks**: Follow the 20-20-20 rule to reduce eye strain and blue light exposure.

- **Do limit screen time before bed**: Avoid using screens at least an hour before bedtime.

- **Do use blue light filter apps**: Install apps that adjust the color temperature of your screens.

- **Do optimize lighting in your environment**: Use dim, warm-colored lights in the evening.

Don'ts:

- **Don't ignore screen brightness**: High brightness levels can increase blue light exposure and eye strain.

- **Don't use screens before bed**: Screen use before bedtime can disrupt sleep patterns.

- **Don't neglect breaks**: Regular breaks are essential to reduce digital eye strain.

- **Don't overlook the importance of blue light filters**: Use filters and glasses to protect your eyes.

- **Don't expose yourself to bright lights in the evening**: Dim lighting can help prepare your body for sleep.

- **Don't forget to monitor your screen time**: Be mindful of your overall screen usage and set limits.

FAQ: Blue Light Filters

Q: WHAT IS BLUE LIGHT, and why is it harmful? A: Blue light is a high-energy visible light with short wavelengths. While it is beneficial during the day, excessive exposure, especially at night, can disrupt sleep patterns and contribute to digital eye strain.

Q: How do blue light filters work? A: Blue light filters reduce the amount of blue light emitted by screens. They can be built into devices, available as apps, or integrated into blue light blocking glasses.

Q: Can blue light exposure really affect sleep? A: Yes, research shows that blue light exposure in the evening can suppress melatonin production, making it harder to fall asleep and reducing sleep quality.

Q: Are blue light blocking glasses effective? A: Studies have shown that blue light blocking glasses can reduce digital eye strain and improve sleep quality. They are particularly useful for individuals who spend long hours in front of screens.

Q: How often should I take breaks to reduce blue light exposure? A: Follow the 20-20-20 rule: every 20 minutes, look at something 20 feet away for at least 20 seconds. This helps reduce eye strain and gives your eyes a break from blue light exposure.

Q: What are some good practices for reducing blue light exposure before bed? A: Avoid using screens at least an hour before bedtime, use built-in blue light filters or blue light blocking glasses, and engage in relaxing activities like reading a book or practicing mindfulness.

Q: Are there specific apps that can help filter blue light? A: Yes, apps like f.lux, Twilight, and Iris can adjust the color temperature of your screens based on the time of day, reducing blue light exposure in the evening.

Q: How can I optimize lighting in my environment to reduce blue light exposure? A: Use dim, warm-colored lights in the evening, and consider LED bulbs with lower color temperatures to minimize blue light emissions.

Case Studies and Examples

KRISTINA'S IMPROVED SLEEP Quality Kristina, a graphic designer, often struggled with falling asleep after late-night work sessions on her computer. She started using her laptop's built-in blue light filter, enabled Night Shift on her phone, and began wearing blue light blocking glasses in the evening. Kristina also adjusted her screen brightness to match the ambient light. Within a few weeks, she noticed significant improvements in her sleep quality and felt more rested in the mornings.

John's Experience with Digital Eye Strain John, a software developer, spent long hours coding and frequently experienced digital eye strain. He invested in blue light blocking glasses and began using the 20-20-20 rule to take regular breaks. John also installed f.lux on his computer to adjust the color temperature based on the time of day. These changes helped alleviate his eye strain and improved his overall comfort while working.

Melody's Bedtime Routine Melody, a writer, found that using her tablet before bed was affecting her sleep. She decided to create a screen-free bedtime routine by reading physical books and practicing relaxation techniques like deep breathing and meditation. Melody also used warm-colored LED bulbs in her bedroom to reduce blue light exposure. These adjustments helped her fall asleep more easily and improved her sleep quality.

Mark's Optimized Workspace Mark, a project manager, worked in an office with bright fluorescent lighting and frequently experienced glare on his computer screen. He installed an anti-reflective screen protector and adjusted his screen brightness to match the ambient light. Mark also used blue light blocking glasses and took regular breaks to rest his eyes. These changes reduced his eye strain and improved his productivity at work.

Emily's Family Blue Light Management Emily, a mother of three, noticed that her children were having trouble falling asleep after using their tablets in the evening. She implemented a family rule to turn off screens an hour before bedtime and encouraged her children to engage in relaxing activities like reading or drawing. Emily also installed blue light filter apps on their devices and used warm-colored lights in their bedrooms. These changes helped improve her children's sleep patterns and overall well-being.

Conclusion

BLUE LIGHT EXPOSURE is an important consideration for maintaining digital wellness and overall health. By using built-in blue light filters, investing in blue light blocking glasses, adjusting screen brightness and contrast, taking regular breaks, limiting screen time before bed, using blue light filter apps, and optimizing lighting in your environment, you can protect your eyes and improve your sleep quality. Implement these strategies to reduce the adverse effects of blue light and enhance your digital experience.

Chapter 7: Enforcing Tech Boundaries

T*he Guarded Gate*

A seeker came to the master and asked, "How can I prevent technology from overwhelming my life?"

The master took the seeker to a garden surrounded by a high wall with a single gate. "Watch," the master said, as they stood by the gate.

The gatekeeper allowed visitors to enter the garden one by one, while politely turning away the crowds. The garden remained peaceful and serene.

The master then said, "Your mind is like this garden, and technology is the crowd. Without boundaries, the crowd will overwhelm and trample the peace within. You must be the gatekeeper."

The seeker asked, "How can I be a good gatekeeper?"

The master replied, "Set times for opening and closing the gate, allow only what is necessary, and keep the rest at bay."

The seeker understood and began to set boundaries for technology use, finding peace and balance in their life.

Introduction

IN AN INCREASINGLY digital world, it's essential to set and maintain healthy boundaries with technology. Without proper tech boundaries, the constant connectivity can lead to stress, burnout, and a diminished quality of life. This chapter explores strategies for enforcing tech boundaries to improve work-life balance and enhance personal interactions.

Understanding Tech Boundaries

TECH BOUNDARIES REFER to the intentional limits set on the use of digital devices and technology to ensure they don't negatively impact your mental and physical health, relationships, or productivity. Dr. Larry Rosen, a psychologist specializing in technology use, emphasizes that setting tech boundaries is crucial for maintaining mental health and well-being in our digitally saturated lives.

Expert Insights and Research

RESEARCH FROM THE *American Psychological Association* indicates that constant connectivity can lead to increased stress and anxiety. The study highlights that individuals who set clear tech boundaries experience lower levels of stress and improved mental health.

A study conducted by the *Pew Research Center* found that while technology can facilitate communication and productivity, it can also blur the lines between work and personal life, leading to burnout. The study suggests that setting boundaries around tech use can help maintain a healthier balance.

Sherry Turkle, a professor at MIT and author of *Reclaiming Conversation: The Power of Talk in a Digital Age,* explains that face-to-face interactions are crucial for building meaningful relationships. Turkle's research shows that excessive use of digital devices can hinder these interactions and negatively impact our social connections.

Practical Steps and Tips

1. DESIGNATE TECH-FREE Zones Create specific areas in your home where digital devices are not allowed. Common tech-free zones include the dining room, bedroom, and living room. This helps create physical boundaries that reinforce your intention to limit tech use in these spaces.

2. Set Tech-Free Times Establish specific times during the day when you will refrain from using digital devices. This could include mealtimes, the first hour after waking up, or the last hour before bed.

Setting these boundaries can help reduce screen time and improve your overall well-being.

3. Use Do Not Disturb Mode Most smartphones have a Do Not Disturb mode that silences notifications and calls. Use this feature during focused work sessions, meetings, or personal time to minimize interruptions. Dr. Larry Rosen recommends scheduling regular periods of tech-free time to prevent digital overload.

4. Limit Social Media Use Set specific times for checking social media and stick to them. Avoid mindless scrolling by setting time limits on social media apps. Tools like Screen Time on iOS or Digital Wellbeing on Android can help you monitor and manage your usage.

5. Create a Digital Curfew Implement a digital curfew where all devices are turned off at a specific time each evening. This can help improve sleep quality by reducing exposure to blue light and creating a relaxing pre-sleep routine. Dr. Charles Czeisler's research highlights the importance of reducing screen time before bed to improve sleep.

6. Communicate Your Boundaries Inform friends, family, and colleagues about your tech boundaries. Clear communication can help manage expectations and ensure that others respect your limits. Dr. Sherry Turkle emphasizes that open communication is key to maintaining healthy relationships in a digital age.

7. Use Apps to Manage Tech Use There are several apps available that can help you enforce tech boundaries. Apps like Freedom, Moment, and Offtime can block distracting apps and websites, track your screen time, and remind you to take breaks. These tools can support your efforts to maintain healthy tech habits.

Additional Tips for Enforcing Tech Boundaries

1. ESTABLISH WORK-LIFE Balance Set clear boundaries between work and personal life. Designate specific work hours and avoid checking work emails or messages outside of these hours. This can help prevent burnout and ensure that you have time for personal activities and relationships.

2. Prioritize Face-to-Face Interactions Make a conscious effort to prioritize in-person interactions over digital communication.

Schedule regular meetups with friends and family, and use video calls instead of text messages for more meaningful connections.

3. Practice Mindfulness Incorporate mindfulness practices into your daily routine to help manage stress and stay present. Techniques such as meditation, deep breathing, and yoga can enhance your ability to focus and reduce the urge to constantly check your devices.

4. Use a Planner Keep track of your tech-free times and activities using a planner or digital calendar. Scheduling tech-free activities can help you stay committed to your boundaries and ensure that you allocate time for important tasks and relationships.

5. Reflect and Adjust Regularly assess your tech boundaries and their effectiveness. Reflect on how your tech use affects your well-being and make adjustments as needed. This ongoing process can help you maintain a healthy balance and adapt to changing circumstances.

Do's and Don'ts of Enforcing Tech Boundaries

DO'S:

• **Do designate tech-free zones**: Create areas in your home where digital devices are not allowed.

• **Do set tech-free times**: Establish specific times during the day to refrain from using digital devices.

• **Do use Do Not Disturb mode**: Minimize interruptions by using Do Not Disturb mode during focused work sessions and personal time.

• **Do limit social media use**: Set specific times for checking social media and stick to them.

• **Do create a digital curfew**: Implement a digital curfew to improve sleep quality and create a relaxing pre-sleep routine.

• **Do communicate your boundaries**: Inform friends, family, and colleagues about your tech boundaries.

- **Do use apps to manage tech use**: Utilize apps that help you enforce tech boundaries and track your screen time.

Don'ts:

- **Don't ignore the importance of tech boundaries**: Setting boundaries is crucial for maintaining mental health and well-being.

- **Don't use devices in tech-free zones**: Stick to your designated tech-free areas to reinforce your boundaries.

- **Don't allow work to invade personal time**: Set clear boundaries between work and personal life.

- **Don't neglect face-to-face interactions**: Prioritize in-person interactions over digital communication.

- **Don't ignore the impact of tech use on sleep**: Reduce screen time before bed to improve sleep quality.

- **Don't forget to reflect and adjust**: Regularly assess your tech boundaries and make adjustments as needed.

FAQ: Enforcing Tech Boundaries

Q: WHY ARE TECH BOUNDARIES important? A: Tech boundaries help prevent digital overload, reduce stress, and improve work-life balance. They ensure that technology use does not negatively impact your mental and physical health, relationships, or productivity.

Q: How do I start setting tech boundaries? A: Begin by designating tech-free zones, setting tech-free times, and using Do Not Disturb mode. Communicate your boundaries with others and use apps to manage your tech use.

Q: What are tech-free zones? A: Tech-free zones are specific areas in your home where digital devices are not allowed. Common tech-free zones include the dining room, bedroom, and living room.

Q: How can I limit social media use? A: Set specific times for checking social media, use tools like Screen Time or Digital

Wellbeing to monitor your usage, and avoid mindless scrolling by setting time limits on social media apps.

Q: What is a digital curfew? A: A digital curfew is a designated time each evening when all devices are turned off. This can help reduce exposure to blue light, improve sleep quality, and create a relaxing pre-sleep routine.

Q: How can I communicate my tech boundaries to others? A: Inform friends, family, and colleagues about your tech boundaries through clear communication. Explain the reasons for your boundaries and ask for their support in respecting them.

Q: Are there apps that can help manage tech use? A: Yes, apps like Freedom, Moment, and Offtime can block distracting apps and websites, track your screen time, and remind you to take breaks. These tools can support your efforts to maintain healthy tech habits.

Q: How do I establish a work-life balance? A: Set clear boundaries between work and personal life by designating specific work hours and avoiding work-related tasks outside of these hours. Prioritize personal activities and relationships to maintain a healthy balance.

Case Studies and Examples

DIANA'S TECH-FREE Zones Diana, a graphic designer, struggled with constantly checking her phone during family meals. She decided to create tech-free zones in her home, including the dining room and bedroom. By enforcing these boundaries, Diana was able to improve her family interactions and reduce her screen time in the evenings, leading to better sleep quality.

John's Digital Curfew John, a software developer, often worked late into the night and found it difficult to unwind before bed. He implemented a digital curfew, turning off all devices an hour before bedtime. John used this time to read, meditate, and engage in relaxation techniques. As a result, he experienced improved sleep quality and felt more rested in the mornings.

Rachel's Work-Life Balance Rachel, a marketing manager, found that her work was invading her personal time, causing burnout. She set clear work hours and communicated her boundaries to her team. Rachel also used Do Not Disturb mode during personal time to minimize interruptions. These changes helped Rachel achieve a healthier work-life balance and reduced her stress levels.

Mark's Social Media Limits Mark, a college student, noticed that he was spending excessive time on social media, affecting his academic performance. He set specific times for checking social media and used Screen Time to monitor his usage. Mark also engaged in mindfulness practices to stay present and focused. These adjustments helped Mark improve his productivity and reduce stress.

Christine's Family Tech Boundaries Christine, a mother of two, observed that her family was spending too much time on screens, leading to reduced quality time together. She established a family digital curfew and designated tech-free zones in their home. Christine also encouraged outdoor activities and face-to-face interactions. These boundaries helped her family reconnect and improved their overall well-being.

Conclusion

ENFORCING TECH BOUNDARIES is essential for maintaining a healthy balance between digital device usage and personal well-being. By designating tech-free zones, setting tech-free times, using Do Not Disturb mode, limiting social media use, creating a digital curfew, communicating your boundaries, and using apps to manage tech use, you can reduce digital overload and improve your quality of life. Implement these strategies to create a healthier relationship with technology and enhance your overall well-being.

Chapter 8: Focus-Boosting Apps You Must Try

T*he Painter's Brush*

A young artist approached the master and asked, "How can I enhance my focus amidst endless distractions?"

The master handed the artist a brush and said, "Paint a single stroke on the canvas without lifting the brush."

The artist, concentrating deeply, painted a long, continuous stroke. When finished, the artist felt a sense of clarity and focus.

The master then said, "The brush is your tool, like focus-boosting apps. It channels your energy and attention into a single, uninterrupted flow. But remember, the tool alone is not enough; it is your intent and discipline that guide the stroke."

The artist asked, "How can I choose the right tools?"

The master replied, "Choose tools that align with your purpose and help maintain your focus. Just as the brush helps you paint, let the right apps guide your attention."

The artist understood and began using focus-boosting apps, finding that their creativity and productivity flourished in the disciplined flow of their work.

Introduction

IN A WORLD FILLED WITH distractions, maintaining focus can be challenging. Fortunately, technology offers solutions in the form of focus-boosting apps designed to help you stay on task and maximize productivity. This chapter explores a selection of apps that can enhance your focus and productivity, providing practical tips for integrating them into your daily routine.

Understanding Focus-Boosting Apps

FOCUS-BOOSTING APPS are designed to help users maintain concentration, manage tasks, and reduce distractions. These apps can range from simple timers and task managers to more complex tools that incorporate mindfulness and behavior-tracking features. Dr. Gloria Mark from the University of California, Irvine, explains that using these apps can significantly improve your ability to stay focused and productive.

Expert Insights and Research

RESEARCH PUBLISHED in the *Journal of Consumer Research* indicates that using productivity apps can help individuals manage their time more effectively and reduce the cognitive load associated with multitasking. The study found that participants who used focus-boosting apps reported higher levels of productivity and lower levels of stress.

Dr. Adam Gazzaley, a neuroscientist and author of *The Distracted Mind*, emphasizes that digital tools, when used appropriately, can enhance cognitive performance. Gazzaley's research shows that focus-boosting apps can help users develop better attention control and reduce the impact of digital distractions.

Recommended Focus-Boosting Apps

1. FOREST Forest is a unique focus-boosting app that encourages users to stay off their phones by growing virtual trees. When you start a focus session, a tree is planted, and it grows as long as you stay focused. If you leave the app, the tree dies. This gamified approach to productivity helps users stay engaged and motivated to complete tasks.

2. Focus@Will Focus@Will is a music app designed to improve concentration by providing scientifically optimized music tracks. The app offers various genres and styles of music that are specifically curated to enhance focus and reduce distractions. Research published in the *Journal of the Acoustical Society of America* supports the use of music for improving cognitive performance.

3. Todoist Todoist is a powerful task management app that helps users organize their tasks and projects. The app allows you to create to-do lists, set deadlines, and prioritize tasks. Dr. Gloria Mark highlights that using task management apps like Todoist can help reduce cognitive overload and improve productivity.

4. Freedom Freedom is an app that blocks distracting websites and apps across all your devices. You can customize your blocklists and schedule focus sessions to minimize digital distractions. The *Journal of Consumer Research* study found that using apps like Freedom can significantly reduce the temptation to engage in distracting activities.

5. Headspace Headspace is a mindfulness and meditation app that offers guided sessions to help users manage stress and improve focus. Incorporating mindfulness practices into your routine can enhance your ability to stay present and concentrate on tasks. Research published in the *Journal of Occupational Health Psychology* shows that mindfulness can improve cognitive function and reduce stress.

6. Pomodone Pomodone integrates the Pomodoro Technique with task management features, allowing users to break their work into focused intervals followed by short breaks. The Pomodoro Technique, developed by Francesco Cirillo, is a time management method that improves productivity by promoting sustained focus and regular breaks.

7. Trello Trello is a visual project management tool that uses boards, lists, and cards to help users organize tasks and collaborate with others. The app's intuitive interface makes it easy to track progress and stay on top of projects. Dr. Adam Gazzaley's research supports the use of visual aids for enhancing focus and productivity.

Practical Steps and Tips

1. IDENTIFY YOUR NEEDS Before choosing a focus-boosting app, identify your specific needs and challenges. Consider whether you need help managing tasks, reducing distractions, or incorporating mindfulness practices. Understanding your needs will help you select the most suitable app.

2. Set Clear Goals Establish clear goals for using focus-boosting apps. Determine what you want to achieve, such as completing specific tasks, improving concentration, or reducing stress. Setting goals will help you stay motivated and track your progress.

3. Customize App Settings Most focus-boosting apps offer customizable settings to suit your preferences. Adjust notifications, themes, and other features to create an optimal user experience. Customizing settings can enhance the app's effectiveness and ensure it meets your needs.

4. Integrate Apps into Your Routine Incorporate focus-boosting apps into your daily routine. Schedule regular focus sessions, use task management tools to organize your day, and set reminders for mindfulness practices. Consistent use of these apps can help you develop better focus habits.

5. Monitor Your Progress Regularly review your progress and assess the effectiveness of the apps you are using. Track your productivity, task completion, and overall well-being. Monitoring your progress can help you identify areas for improvement and adjust your strategies as needed.

6. Combine Multiple Apps Consider using a combination of focus-boosting apps to address different aspects of productivity. For example, you might use Forest to stay off your phone, Todoist to manage tasks, and Headspace for mindfulness practices. Combining multiple apps can provide a comprehensive approach to improving focus.

Additional Tips for Enhancing Focus

1. CREATE A DISTRACTION-Free Environment Ensure your workspace is free from distractions. Minimize clutter, use noise-canceling headphones, and create a designated work area. A distraction-free environment can enhance the effectiveness of focus-boosting apps.

2. Practice Mindfulness Incorporate mindfulness practices into your routine to improve focus and reduce stress. Techniques such as meditation, deep breathing, and mindful breaks can help you stay present and concentrated.

3. Take Regular Breaks Follow the Pomodoro Technique or similar methods to take regular breaks. Short breaks can help prevent burnout and maintain your energy levels throughout the day. Use apps like Pomodone to schedule these breaks effectively.

4. Prioritize Tasks Use task management apps to prioritize your tasks and focus on the most important ones first. Breaking down large projects into smaller, manageable tasks can help you stay organized and motivated.

5. Set Boundaries Establish clear boundaries between work and personal time. Use apps like Freedom to block distracting websites during work hours and ensure that you have dedicated time for focused work.

Do's and Don'ts of Using Focus-Boosting Apps
DO'S:

- **Do identify your needs**: Understand your specific challenges and choose apps that address them.

- **Do set clear goals**: Establish goals for using focus-boosting apps to stay motivated and track progress.

- **Do customize app settings**: Adjust settings to create an optimal user experience.

- **Do integrate apps into your routine**: Consistently use focus-boosting apps as part of your daily routine.

- **Do monitor your progress**: Regularly review your productivity and well-being to assess the effectiveness of the apps.

- **Do combine multiple apps**: Use a combination of apps to address different aspects of productivity.

- **Do create a distraction-free environment**: Minimize distractions in your workspace to enhance focus.

Don'ts:

- **Don't rely solely on apps**: Focus-boosting apps are tools to support your efforts, not a substitute for good habits.

- **Don't ignore customization**: Tailoring app settings to your preferences can enhance their effectiveness.

- **Don't skip breaks**: Regular breaks are essential for maintaining focus and preventing burnout.

- **Don't neglect mindfulness**: Incorporate mindfulness practices to improve focus and reduce stress.

- **Don't overlook task prioritization**: Use task management apps to prioritize and organize your tasks.

- **Don't ignore boundaries**: Establish clear boundaries between work and personal time to maintain balance.

FAQ: Focus-Boosting Apps

Q: WHAT ARE FOCUS-BOOSTING apps? A: Focus-boosting apps are digital tools designed to help users maintain concentration, manage tasks, and reduce distractions. They can range from simple timers and task managers to more complex tools that incorporate mindfulness and behavior-tracking features.

Q: How do focus-boosting apps improve productivity? A: These apps provide structure, reduce distractions, and help users manage their time effectively. By promoting sustained focus and regular breaks, they can enhance cognitive performance and overall productivity.

Q: What are some popular focus-boosting apps? A: Popular focus-boosting apps include Forest, Focus@Will, Todoist, Freedom, Headspace, Pomodone, and Trello. Each app offers unique features to help users stay focused and productive.

Q: How do I choose the right focus-boosting app? A: Identify your specific needs and challenges, such as managing tasks, reducing distractions, or incorporating mindfulness practices. Choose an app that addresses these needs and offers customizable settings.

Q: Can I use multiple focus-boosting apps simultaneously? A: Yes, using a combination of apps can provide a comprehensive approach to improving focus. For example, you might use Forest to stay off your phone, Todoist to manage tasks, and Headspace for mindfulness practices.

Q: How often should I use focus-boosting apps? A: Integrate these apps into your daily routine and use them consistently. Schedule regular focus sessions, use task management tools to organize your day, and set reminders for mindfulness practices.

Q: Are focus-boosting apps suitable for all types of work? A: Yes, focus-boosting apps can be beneficial for various types of work, including creative, administrative, and technical tasks. They help create structure and reduce distractions, enhancing overall productivity.

Q: How can I monitor my progress with focus-boosting apps? A: Track your productivity, task completion, and overall well-being using the app's built-in features or a separate planner. Regularly review your progress and adjust your strategies as needed.

Case Studies and Examples

SOPHIA'S USE OF FOREST Sophia, a graphic designer, often found herself distracted by her phone during work hours. She started using Forest to stay off her phone and focus on her tasks. By growing virtual trees during her focus sessions, Sophia felt more motivated to complete her work and enjoyed the gamified approach to productivity. As a result, she noticed a significant improvement in her focus and task completion.

John's Experience with Focus@Will John, a software developer, struggled to concentrate in a noisy office environment. He began using Focus@Will to listen to scientifically optimized music tracks while working. The app's music helped John block out distractions and maintain his focus. He reported increased productivity and a more enjoyable work experience.

Rachel's Task Management with Todoist Rachel, a marketing manager, felt overwhelmed by her workload and struggled to keep track of tasks. She started using Todoist to organize her tasks and set priorities. The app's intuitive interface and task management features helped Rachel stay on top of her projects and reduce cognitive overload. She experienced improved productivity and reduced stress.

Mark's Digital Detox with Freedom Mark, a college student, found himself frequently distracted by social media and other websites while studying. He installed Freedom to block distracting websites and apps during study sessions. By limiting digital distractions, Mark was able to focus better on his coursework and improve his academic performance.

Tanya's Mindfulness Practice with Headspace Tanya, a product manager, often felt stressed and unfocused at work. She incorporated Headspace into her daily routine to practice mindfulness and meditation. The guided sessions helped Tanya manage her stress and stay present during work hours. She reported improved focus, reduced stress, and better overall well-being.

Conclusion

FOCUS-BOOSTING APPS are valuable tools for enhancing productivity and maintaining concentration in a world filled with distractions. By identifying your needs, setting clear goals, customizing app settings, integrating apps into your routine, monitoring your progress, and combining multiple apps, you can effectively use these tools to improve your focus and productivity. Implement these strategies to harness the power of focus-boosting apps and achieve your goals more efficiently.

Chapter 9: Digital Ergonomics: The New Essentials

The Comfortable Seat

A novice, troubled by aches from long hours at the desk, asked the master, "How can I work without discomfort?"

The master led the novice to a room with two chairs. One was hard and rigid, the other soft and well-cushioned. "Sit in each chair," the master instructed.

The novice sat in the hard chair first, feeling the discomfort almost immediately. Then, they sat in the soft chair and felt at ease.

The master asked, "Which chair allows you to sit longer with ease?"

The novice replied, "The soft, well-cushioned chair."

The master nodded, "Your workspace should be like the comfortable chair. It should support you and reduce strain, allowing you to work with ease. Adjust your tools and surroundings to fit you, not the other way around."

The novice understood and began setting up their workspace with proper ergonomics, finding comfort and increased productivity in their tasks.

Introduction

IN AN ERA WHERE MANY of us spend countless hours in front of screens, digital ergonomics has become an essential aspect of maintaining health and productivity. Poor ergonomic practices can lead to a host of physical issues, including musculoskeletal pain, eye strain, and fatigue. This chapter delves into the principles of digital ergonomics and provides practical strategies to create a healthier and more comfortable workspace.

Understanding Digital Ergonomics

DIGITAL ERGONOMICS involves designing a workspace and adopting practices that minimize physical strain and enhance comfort while using digital devices. Dr. Alan Hedge, a professor of ergonomics at Cornell University, explains that proper ergonomic practices can prevent repetitive strain injuries and improve overall well-being.

Expert Insights and Research

RESEARCH PUBLISHED in the *Journal of Occupational Rehabilitation* highlights the importance of ergonomic interventions in reducing workplace injuries and improving productivity. The study found that individuals who adopted ergonomic practices experienced fewer musculoskeletal issues and reported higher job satisfaction.

The Occupational Safety and Health Administration (OSHA) emphasizes the need for ergonomic workplace design to prevent injuries. OSHA's guidelines include recommendations for proper workstation setup, posture, and the use of ergonomic accessories.

Dr. David Rempel from the University of California, Berkeley, has conducted extensive research on the impact of ergonomics on health and productivity. His studies show that ergonomic interventions can significantly reduce the risk of developing musculoskeletal disorders and improve work performance.

Practical Steps and Tips

1. OPTIMIZE YOUR CHAIR A good chair is the foundation of an ergonomic workspace. Choose a chair that supports your lower back and allows your feet to rest flat on the floor. Adjust the seat height so your knees are at a 90-degree angle, and ensure that the chair provides adequate lumbar support. Dr. Alan Hedge recommends using an adjustable chair that can be tailored to your body and work requirements.

2. Position Your Monitor Correctly Your monitor should be at eye level and about 20-30 inches away from your face. The top of the screen should be at or slightly below eye level to prevent neck strain. The American Optometric Association suggests positioning your monitor to avoid glare and reduce eye strain.

3. Use an Ergonomic Keyboard and Mouse An ergonomic keyboard and mouse can help reduce strain on your wrists and hands. Look for keyboards with a slight negative tilt and mice that fit comfortably in your hand. Dr. David Rempel emphasizes the importance of keeping your wrists in a neutral position to prevent repetitive strain injuries.

4. Maintain Proper Posture Good posture is crucial for preventing musculoskeletal pain. Sit with your back straight, shoulders relaxed, and elbows at a 90-degree angle. Avoid slouching or leaning forward. The Mayo Clinic suggests using a small pillow or lumbar roll to support your lower back and maintain proper posture.

5. Take Regular Breaks Taking regular breaks is essential for preventing fatigue and strain. Follow the 20-20-20 rule: every 20 minutes, look at something 20 feet away for at least 20 seconds. Additionally, stand up, stretch, and move around every hour to improve circulation and reduce muscle tension.

6. Arrange Your Desk for Comfort Organize your desk to keep frequently used items within easy reach. Avoid clutter and ensure that your workspace is well-lit. The American Physical Therapy Association recommends using a document holder to place reading materials at the same height as your monitor, reducing the need for frequent eye and neck movements.

7. Use Ergonomic Accessories Consider using ergonomic accessories like monitor stands, footrests, and wrist supports to enhance your comfort. These tools can help you maintain proper posture and reduce the risk of developing musculoskeletal issues. Dr. Alan Hedge advises selecting accessories that can be adjusted to fit your individual needs.

Additional Tips for Digital Ergonomics

1. INCORPORATE MOVEMENT into Your Routine
Incorporate regular movement into your workday to prevent stiffness and improve overall health. Simple exercises like neck rolls, shoulder shrugs, and leg stretches can alleviate tension and promote blood flow. The Mayo Clinic suggests using a standing desk or desk

converter to alternate between sitting and standing throughout the day.

2. Adjust Your Screen Settings Adjust your screen settings to reduce glare and eye strain. Increase the text size and adjust the contrast to make content easier to read. The American Academy of Ophthalmology recommends using screen filters or anti-glare coatings to minimize reflections and improve visual comfort.

3. Practice Eye Care In addition to the 20-20-20 rule, practice other eye care techniques to maintain eye health. Blink frequently to keep your eyes moist, and use artificial tears if needed. Schedule regular eye exams to monitor and address any vision issues related to screen use.

4. Use Voice Recognition Software Consider using voice recognition software to reduce the need for typing. This can help alleviate strain on your wrists and hands. Software like Dragon NaturallySpeaking allows you to dictate text and control your computer using voice commands, reducing the risk of repetitive strain injuries.

5. Stay Hydrated Staying hydrated is essential for maintaining overall health, including eye health. Drink plenty of water throughout the day to keep your eyes and body hydrated. Proper hydration can help reduce fatigue and improve concentration.

Do's and Don'ts of Digital Ergonomics

DO'S:

- **Do use an adjustable chair**: Ensure your chair provides adequate lumbar support and can be adjusted to your needs.

- **Do position your monitor correctly**: Place your monitor at eye level and about 20-30 inches away from your face.

- **Do use an ergonomic keyboard and mouse**: Choose devices that reduce strain on your wrists and hands.

- **Do maintain proper posture**: Sit with your back straight, shoulders relaxed, and elbows at a 90-degree angle.

- **Do take regular breaks**: Follow the 20-20-20 rule and stand up, stretch, and move around every hour.

- **Do arrange your desk for comfort**: Keep frequently used items within easy reach and ensure your workspace is well-lit.

- **Do use ergonomic accessories**: Consider using monitor stands, footrests, and wrist supports to enhance comfort.

- **Do incorporate movement into your routine**: Perform simple exercises to alleviate tension and improve blood flow.

- **Do adjust your screen settings**: Reduce glare and eye strain by adjusting text size, contrast, and using screen filters.

- **Do practice eye care**: Follow the 20-20-20 rule, blink frequently, and schedule regular eye exams.

- **Do use voice recognition software**: Reduce typing strain by using voice commands to control your computer.

- **Do stay hydrated**: Drink plenty of water to maintain overall health and reduce fatigue.

Don'ts:

- **Don't use a non-adjustable chair**: Ensure your chair can be adjusted to fit your needs and provides proper support.

- **Don't position your monitor too high or low**: Place your monitor at eye level to prevent neck strain.

- **Don't ignore ergonomic accessories**: Use tools like wrist supports and footrests to enhance comfort.

- **Don't neglect breaks**: Regular breaks are essential to prevent fatigue and strain.

- **Don't slouch or lean forward**: Maintain proper posture to reduce the risk of musculoskeletal issues.

- **Don't overlook eye care**: Practice eye care techniques to maintain visual health.

- **Don't allow clutter to accumulate**: Keep your workspace organized and free from distractions.

- **Don't ignore the importance of hydration**: Staying hydrated is crucial for maintaining health and productivity.

- **Don't rely solely on typing**: Use voice recognition software to reduce the risk of repetitive strain injuries.

- **Don't forget to move**: Incorporate regular movement into your workday to prevent stiffness and improve overall health.

FAQ: Digital Ergonomics

Q: WHAT IS DIGITAL ergonomics? A: Digital ergonomics involves designing a workspace and adopting practices that minimize physical strain and enhance comfort while using digital devices. Proper ergonomic practices can prevent repetitive strain injuries and improve overall well-being.

Q: How do I set up an ergonomic workspace? A: Optimize your chair, position your monitor correctly, use an ergonomic keyboard and mouse, maintain proper posture, take regular breaks, arrange your desk for comfort, and use ergonomic accessories.

Q: Why is posture important in digital ergonomics? A: Good posture prevents musculoskeletal pain and reduces the risk of developing repetitive strain injuries. Sit with your back straight, shoulders relaxed, and elbows at a 90-degree angle to maintain proper posture.

Q: How often should I take breaks to reduce strain? A: Follow the 20-20-20 rule: every 20 minutes, look at something 20 feet away for at least 20 seconds. Additionally, stand up, stretch, and move around every hour to improve circulation and reduce muscle tension.

Q: What are some simple exercises to incorporate into my routine? A: Simple exercises like neck rolls, shoulder shrugs, and leg stretches can alleviate tension and promote blood flow. Using a standing desk or desk converter can also help you alternate between sitting and standing.

Q: How can I reduce eye strain while using screens? A: Adjust your screen settings to reduce glare, increase text size, and adjust contrast. Follow the 20-20-20 rule, blink frequently, and use artificial tears if needed. Schedule regular eye exams to monitor and address any vision issues.

Q: What ergonomic accessories should I consider using? A: Consider using monitor stands, footrests, wrist supports, and screen filters to enhance comfort and reduce strain. These tools can help you maintain proper posture and prevent musculoskeletal issues.

Q: How can voice recognition software help with ergonomics? A: Voice recognition software allows you to dictate text and control your computer using voice commands, reducing the need for typing and alleviating strain on your wrists and hands.

Case Studies and Examples

SOPHIA'S ERGONOMIC Workspace Sophia, a graphic designer, often experienced neck and back pain from long hours at her desk. She invested in an adjustable chair and positioned her monitor at eye level. Sophia also used an ergonomic keyboard and mouse to reduce strain on her wrists. Additionally, she followed the 20-20-20 rule and took regular breaks to stretch. These changes significantly improved her comfort and productivity.

John's Use of Voice Recognition Software John, a software developer, developed repetitive strain injuries from extensive typing. He started using voice recognition software to dictate code and control his computer. John also adjusted his workstation to include an ergonomic chair and monitor stand. These adjustments helped alleviate his wrist pain and improved his overall work experience.

Rachel's Eye Care Routine Rachel, a writer, often experienced eye strain and fatigue from prolonged screen use. She adjusted her screen settings to reduce glare and increase text size. Rachel also followed the 20-20-20 rule and used artificial tears to keep her eyes moist. Regular eye exams helped her monitor and address any vision issues. These practices reduced her eye strain and improved her visual comfort.

Mark's Movement Routine Mark, a project manager, found that sitting for long periods led to stiffness and discomfort. He incorporated regular movement into his workday by using a standing desk converter and performing simple exercises like neck rolls and shoulder shrugs. Mark also took regular breaks to stretch and move around. These practices improved his overall well-being and reduced musculoskeletal pain.

Emily's Hydration and Ergonomics Emily, a customer service representative, often felt fatigued and experienced back pain from her desk job. She ensured she stayed hydrated by drinking water throughout the day. Emily also invested in an ergonomic chair with lumbar support and positioned her monitor at eye level. She incorporated regular breaks and movement into her routine. These changes improved her energy levels and reduced her discomfort.

Conclusion

DIGITAL ERGONOMICS is essential for maintaining health and productivity in a world where many of us spend extended periods in front of screens. By optimizing your chair, positioning your monitor correctly, using ergonomic accessories, maintaining proper posture, taking regular breaks, incorporating movement, adjusting screen settings, practicing eye care, using voice recognition software, and staying hydrated, you can create a healthier and more comfortable workspace. Implement these strategies to enhance your well-being and productivity in the digital age.

Chapter 10: Eye Strain No More: Top Techniques

T *he Gentle Gaze*

A scholar, suffering from tired eyes, asked the sage, "How can I relieve my eye strain from endless reading and screen time?"

The sage took the scholar to a meadow and said, "Gaze at the distant mountains."

The scholar, focusing intently, strained to see the details. The sage then said, "Now, soften your gaze and simply take in the view without effort."

The scholar relaxed and let their eyes rest on the broad scene, feeling a sense of relief.

The sage explained, "Your eyes, like the mind, need moments of rest. When strained, they suffer. Practice the gentle gaze, shifting focus regularly, and let your eyes find peace in balance."

The scholar understood and began practicing techniques to relieve eye strain, such as taking regular breaks, adjusting screen settings, and allowing their eyes to rest. They found their vision clearer and their work more comfortable.

Introduction

WITH THE INCREASING use of digital devices, eye strain has become a common issue affecting many people. Digital eye strain, also known as computer vision syndrome, can cause discomfort and reduce productivity. This chapter explores effective techniques to reduce eye strain and maintain healthy vision in the digital age.

Understanding Digital Eye Strain

DIGITAL EYE STRAIN is a condition characterized by discomfort and visual problems resulting from prolonged use of digital screens. Symptoms include headaches, blurred vision, dry eyes, and neck and shoulder pain. Dr. Jeff Anshel, founder of the Ocular Nutrition Society, emphasizes that understanding and addressing the causes of digital eye strain is crucial for maintaining eye health.

Expert Insights and Research

RESEARCH PUBLISHED in the *Journal of Environmental Psychology* highlights the prevalence of digital eye strain and its impact on productivity. The study found that individuals who implemented eye care techniques experienced fewer symptoms and improved overall comfort.

The American Optometric Association recommends adopting the 20-20-20 rule, using proper lighting, and taking regular breaks to reduce eye strain. Dr. Joshua Dunaief from the University of Pennsylvania emphasizes the importance of regular eye exams to monitor and address any vision issues related to screen use.

Practical Steps and Tips

1. FOLLOW THE 20-20-20 Rule The 20-20-20 rule is a simple and effective technique to reduce eye strain. Every 20 minutes, look at something 20 feet away for at least 20 seconds. This practice helps relax the eye muscles and prevent fatigue.

2. Adjust Screen Brightness and Contrast Ensure that your screen brightness is set to a comfortable level that matches the ambient lighting in your environment. Adjust the contrast to make text and images easier to see. The American Academy of Ophthalmology recommends reducing glare by using screen filters or anti-glare coatings.

3. Use Proper Lighting Avoid working in dimly lit rooms or under harsh fluorescent lights. Use soft, indirect lighting to minimize glare and reflections on your screen. Position your screen to avoid reflections from windows or overhead lights.

4. Blink More Often When focusing on a screen, people tend to blink less frequently, leading to dry eyes. Make a conscious effort to blink more often to keep your eyes moist. The American Optometric Association suggests using artificial tears if needed to alleviate dryness.

5. Take Regular Breaks In addition to following the 20-20-20 rule, take regular breaks to rest your eyes and prevent fatigue. Stand up, stretch, and move around every hour to improve circulation and reduce muscle tension.

6. Adjust Text Size and Color Contrast Increase the text size and adjust the color contrast on your screen to reduce eye strain. Larger text and proper contrast make content easier to read and reduce the need for squinting.

7. Maintain an Ergonomic Setup Position your monitor at eye level, about 20-30 inches away from your face. Ensure that your chair supports your lower back and that your feet are flat on the floor. Proper ergonomics can help reduce neck and shoulder strain associated with screen use.

Additional Tips for Reducing Eye Strain

1. USE BLUE LIGHT FILTERS Blue light from screens can contribute to eye strain and disrupt sleep. Use built-in blue light filters on your devices or install blue light filter apps to reduce exposure. Dr. Lisa Ostrin from the University of Houston recommends using blue light blocking glasses for added protection.

2. Practice Eye Exercises Simple eye exercises can help reduce strain and improve eye health. Try rolling your eyes, focusing on near and far objects, and practicing figure-eight movements. These exercises can strengthen eye muscles and improve flexibility.

3. Stay Hydrated Staying hydrated is essential for maintaining eye health. Drink plenty of water throughout the day to keep your eyes moist and reduce the risk of dryness and irritation.

4. Schedule Regular Eye Exams Regular eye exams are crucial for monitoring and addressing any vision issues related to screen use. Dr. Joshua Dunaief emphasizes the importance of routine check-ups to ensure your eyes are healthy and to catch any problems early.

5. Use Anti-Reflective Screen Protectors Anti-reflective screen protectors can help reduce glare and reflections from your monitor.

These protectors are available for most devices and can significantly improve your viewing experience.

Do's and Don'ts of Reducing Eye Strain
DO'S:

• **Do follow the 20-20-20 rule**: Take regular breaks to rest your eyes.

• **Do adjust screen brightness and contrast**: Ensure your screen is comfortable to look at.

• **Do use proper lighting**: Minimize glare and reflections with soft, indirect lighting.

• **Do blink more often**: Keep your eyes moist by blinking frequently.

• **Do take regular breaks**: Stand up, stretch, and move around to reduce fatigue.

• **Do adjust text size and color contrast**: Make content easier to read to reduce strain.

• **Do maintain an ergonomic setup**: Position your monitor and chair correctly.

• **Do use blue light filters**: Reduce blue light exposure with built-in filters or apps.

• **Do practice eye exercises**: Strengthen and relax your eye muscles with simple exercises.

• **Do stay hydrated**: Drink plenty of water to keep your eyes moist.

• **Do schedule regular eye exams**: Monitor and address vision issues with routine check-ups.

• **Do use anti-reflective screen protectors**: Reduce glare and improve visual comfort.

Don'ts:

• **Don't ignore eye discomfort**: Address any symptoms of eye strain promptly.

• **Don't use screens in dim lighting**: Ensure your workspace is well-lit to reduce strain.

• **Don't neglect breaks**: Regular breaks are essential for maintaining eye health.

• **Don't overlook text size and contrast**: Adjust settings to make content easier to read.

• **Don't forget to blink**: Blinking frequently helps keep your eyes moist.

• **Don't ignore hydration**: Staying hydrated is crucial for eye health.

• **Don't skip eye exams**: Regular check-ups are important for monitoring vision health.

• **Don't rely solely on screen adjustments**: Incorporate other eye care techniques to reduce strain.

FAQ: Reducing Eye Strain

Q: WHAT IS DIGITAL eye strain? A: Digital eye strain, also known as computer vision syndrome, is a condition characterized by discomfort and visual problems resulting from prolonged use of digital screens. Symptoms include headaches, blurred vision, dry eyes, and neck and shoulder pain.

Q: How can I reduce eye strain while using screens? A: Follow the 20-20-20 rule, adjust screen brightness and contrast, use proper lighting, blink more often, take regular breaks, and maintain an ergonomic setup. Additionally, use blue light filters and practice eye exercises to reduce strain.

Q: What is the 20-20-20 rule? A: The 20-20-20 rule is a simple technique to reduce eye strain. Every 20 minutes, look at something 20 feet away for at least 20 seconds. This helps relax the eye muscles and prevent fatigue.

Q: How often should I take breaks to reduce eye strain? A: Take regular breaks every hour to rest your eyes and prevent fatigue. Follow the 20-20-20 rule and stand up, stretch, and move around to improve circulation and reduce muscle tension.

Q: How can blue light filters help with eye strain? A: Blue light filters reduce the amount of blue light emitted by screens, which can contribute to eye strain and disrupt sleep. Use built-in filters or install blue light filter apps, and consider using blue light blocking glasses for added protection.

Q: Why is proper lighting important for reducing eye strain? A: Proper lighting minimizes glare and reflections on your screen, reducing eye strain. Use soft, indirect lighting and position your screen to avoid reflections from windows or overhead lights.

Q: What are some simple eye exercises to reduce strain? A: Try rolling your eyes, focusing on near and far objects, and practicing figure-eight movements. These exercises can strengthen eye muscles and improve flexibility, reducing strain.

Q: How can I keep my eyes moist while using screens? A: Blink frequently to keep your eyes moist, and use artificial tears if needed. Staying hydrated by drinking plenty of water throughout the day also helps maintain eye moisture.

Case Studies and Examples

SOPHIA'S IMPROVED EYE Health Sophia, a software developer, experienced frequent headaches and dry eyes from long hours at her computer. She started following the 20-20-20 rule, adjusted her screen brightness, and used blue light blocking glasses. Sophia also incorporated eye exercises into her routine and stayed hydrated. Within a few weeks, she noticed a significant reduction in eye strain and an improvement in her overall comfort.

John's Ergonomic Setup John, a graphic designer, struggled with neck and shoulder pain due to poor posture and screen glare. He repositioned his monitor to eye level, used an anti-reflective screen protector, and adjusted his chair for better support. John also took regular breaks to stretch and move around. These changes alleviated his discomfort and improved his productivity.

Rachel's Eye Care Routine Rachel, a writer, often experienced blurred vision and eye fatigue. She adjusted the text size and contrast on her screen, used proper lighting, and practiced eye exercises. Rachel also followed the 20-20-20 rule and scheduled regular eye exams. These practices reduced her symptoms and enhanced her visual comfort.

Mark's Use of Blue Light Filters Mark, a college student, had trouble sleeping after late-night study sessions on his laptop. He enabled the blue light filter on his devices, set a digital curfew, and used blue light blocking glasses. Mark also created a relaxing pre-sleep routine that included reading physical books. These adjustments significantly improved his sleep quality and reduced his eye strain.

Emily's Hydration and Eye Exercises Emily, a teacher, often experienced dry eyes and fatigue from preparing lessons on her computer. She started drinking more water throughout the day to stay hydrated and incorporated eye exercises into her routine. Emily also used artificial tears to keep her eyes moist. These changes helped alleviate her dry eyes and improved her overall comfort while working.

David's Screen Adjustment Techniques David, a financial analyst, frequently dealt with eye strain and headaches due to screen glare. He adjusted the brightness and contrast settings on his computer and used an anti-glare screen protector. David also repositioned his monitor to reduce reflections and followed the 20-20-20 rule. These practices significantly reduced his eye strain and improved his productivity.

Lisa's Comprehensive Eye Care Plan Lisa, a marketing professional, experienced persistent eye strain from long hours of digital work. She implemented a comprehensive eye care plan that included adjusting her screen settings, using blue light filters, practicing the 20-20-20 rule, and taking regular breaks. Lisa also scheduled routine eye exams and used anti-reflective screen protectors. This holistic approach helped Lisa maintain healthy vision and reduced her symptoms of digital eye strain.

Michael's Ergonomic Workspace Michael, a data scientist, dealt with neck and shoulder pain along with eye strain. He optimized his workspace by adjusting his chair and monitor for better ergonomics. Michael also increased the text size on his screens and used proper lighting to minimize glare. Additionally, he incorporated regular breaks and eye exercises into his workday. These changes improved Michael's posture, reduced his discomfort, and enhanced his focus.

Conclusion

REDUCING EYE STRAIN is essential for maintaining healthy vision and overall well-being in the digital age. By following the 20-20-20 rule, adjusting screen brightness and contrast, using proper lighting, blinking more often, taking regular breaks, adjusting text size and contrast, maintaining an ergonomic setup, using blue light filters, practicing eye exercises, staying hydrated, scheduling regular eye exams, and using anti-reflective screen protectors, you can effectively reduce eye strain and improve your visual comfort. Implement these techniques to protect your eyes and enhance your productivity in a digital world.

Chapter 11: Transforming Email Management

The Flowing Stream

A busy executive approached the master, frustrated, "My inbox overflows like a torrent, and I cannot keep up. How can I manage this constant flow?"

The master led the executive to a stream. "Watch the water," the master said.

The stream flowed steadily, but occasionally, leaves and branches would gather and slow it down. The master gently removed the debris, and the water flowed smoothly again.

The master turned to the executive and said, "Your email is like this stream. When debris accumulates, it disrupts the flow. Regularly clear the clutter, and it will flow smoothly once more."

The executive asked, "How can I keep it clear?"

The master replied, "Set times for checking, categorize and prioritize, and let the rest go. Maintain the flow with mindful attention, and you will find balance."

The executive understood and began applying these principles to email management, finding a smoother and more manageable flow in their daily work.

Introduction

Email is a powerful communication tool, but it can also become overwhelming if not managed properly. An overflowing inbox can lead to stress, missed messages, and decreased productivity. This chapter explores strategies for transforming your email management to achieve inbox zero, prioritize effectively, and communicate efficiently.

Understanding Email Overload

Email overload occurs when the volume of incoming messages surpasses your ability to manage them effectively. This can lead to feelings of stress and anxiety, as well as decreased productivity. Merlin Mann, the creator of the Inbox Zero concept, emphasizes the importance of maintaining control over your inbox to reduce stress and improve efficiency.

Expert Insights and Research

Research from the *Harvard Business Review* highlights the impact of email overload on productivity. The study found that employees spend an average of 28% of their workweek managing email, which can detract from more important tasks. Implementing effective email management strategies can significantly reduce this burden.

The *Journal of Business Communication* suggests that prioritizing emails and setting clear guidelines for email use can enhance communication efficiency. Dr. Cal Newport, author of *Deep Work*, advocates for structured email practices to minimize disruptions and maintain focus.

Practical Steps and Tips

1. Achieve Inbox Zero Inbox zero is a rigorous approach to email management where your goal is to keep your inbox empty—or almost empty—at all times. Here are some strategies to achieve inbox zero:

- **Process, Don't Procrastinate**: When you open an email, decide immediately whether to delete, delegate, respond, defer, or do it. This helps keep your inbox clear.

- **Use Folders and Labels**: Create folders and labels to organize emails by category, project, or priority. This makes it easier to find important messages and manage your workflow.

- **Unsubscribe Ruthlessly**: Unsubscribe from newsletters and promotional emails that you no longer find useful. This reduces clutter and helps you focus on important emails.

2. Prioritize Effectively Prioritizing your emails ensures that you address the most important messages first. Here are some tips for effective prioritization:

- **Use Flags and Stars**: Many email clients allow you to flag or star important emails. Use these features to mark emails that require immediate attention.

- **Set Up Filters**: Create filters to automatically sort incoming emails into folders based on sender, subject, or keywords. This helps you quickly identify high-priority emails.

- **Batch Process Emails**: Set specific times during the day to check and respond to emails. Avoid constantly checking your inbox, as this can disrupt your workflow.

3. Communicate Efficiently Efficient communication via email can save time and reduce misunderstandings. Here are some strategies for effective email communication:

- **Be Clear and Concise**: Write clear and concise emails. Get to the point quickly and avoid unnecessary details.

- **Use Descriptive Subject Lines**: A descriptive subject line helps the recipient understand the purpose of your email at a glance. This increases the chances of a timely response.

- **Limit Recipients**: Only include necessary recipients in your emails. This reduces clutter and ensures that your message reaches the right people.

4. Use Email Management Tools Several tools can help you manage your emails more effectively. Here are some recommended tools:

- **Boomerang**: Boomerang allows you to schedule emails to be sent later, set reminders for follow-ups, and temporarily archive emails that don't need immediate action.

- **SaneBox**: SaneBox analyzes your email habits and prioritizes important emails. It filters less important emails into separate folders, helping you focus on what matters.

- **Unroll.Me**: Unroll.Me helps you unsubscribe from unwanted emails and consolidates subscription emails into a single daily digest.

Additional Tips for Transforming Email Management

1. Set Email Boundaries Establish clear boundaries for email use to prevent it from taking over your day. Set specific times to check and respond to emails, and avoid checking your inbox outside of these times. Communicate your email boundaries to colleagues and clients to manage their expectations.

2. Create Email Templates Create templates for common email responses to save time and ensure consistency. Use templates for frequently asked questions, meeting requests, and follow-ups. Customize each template as needed to personalize your responses.

3. Archive and Delete Regularly Regularly archive or delete old emails to keep your inbox manageable. Use your email client's archiving features to store important emails in separate folders, and delete emails that are no longer needed.

4. Use the Two-Minute Rule If an email can be addressed in two minutes or less, handle it immediately. This helps prevent small tasks from piling up and keeps your inbox clear.

Do's and Don'ts of Email Management
Do's:

- **Do aim for inbox zero**: Keep your inbox empty or almost empty by processing emails promptly.

- **Do prioritize effectively**: Use flags, stars, and filters to identify high-priority emails.

- **Do communicate efficiently**: Write clear and concise emails with descriptive subject lines.

- **Do use email management tools**: Leverage tools like Boomerang, SaneBox, and Unroll.Me to streamline your email management.

- **Do set email boundaries**: Establish specific times to check and respond to emails.

- **Do create email templates**: Save time by using templates for common responses.

- **Do archive and delete regularly**: Keep your inbox manageable by archiving or deleting old emails.

- **Do use the two-minute rule**: Handle emails that can be addressed quickly to prevent small tasks from piling up.

Don'ts:

- **Don't procrastinate**: Process emails promptly to maintain control over your inbox.

- **Don't ignore email boundaries**: Avoid checking your inbox outside of designated times.

- **Don't over-communicate**: Limit recipients to those who need to see your email.

- **Don't neglect prioritization**: Identify and address high-priority emails first.

- **Don't forget to unsubscribe**: Reduce clutter by unsubscribing from unwanted emails.

- **Don't hoard emails**: Regularly archive or delete emails to keep your inbox clear.

FAQ: Email Management

Q: What is inbox zero? A: Inbox zero is an email management strategy where the goal is to keep your inbox empty or almost empty at all times by processing emails promptly and effectively.

Q: How can I prioritize my emails effectively? A: Use flags and stars to mark important emails, set up filters to sort incoming messages, and batch process emails at specific times during the day to manage your workflow.

Q: What are some tools that can help with email management? A: Tools like Boomerang, SaneBox, and Unroll.Me can help you schedule emails, prioritize important messages, and reduce clutter by managing subscriptions.

Q: How can I communicate more efficiently via email? A: Write clear and concise emails, use descriptive subject lines, and limit recipients to those who need to see your message. Create templates for common responses to save time.

Q: What is the two-minute rule for email management? A: The two-minute rule suggests that if an email can be addressed in two minutes or less, handle it immediately. This helps prevent small tasks from piling up and keeps your inbox clear.

Case Studies and Examples

Sophia's Inbox Zero Transformation Sophia, a project manager, often felt overwhelmed by her overflowing inbox. She implemented the inbox zero strategy by processing emails promptly and using folders and labels to organize her messages. Sophia also unsubscribed from unwanted emails and used Boomerang to schedule follow-ups. These changes helped Sophia maintain an empty inbox and reduced her email-related stress.

John's Efficient Email Communication John, a sales executive, struggled with long email threads and delayed responses. He started writing clear and concise emails with descriptive subject lines. John also set specific times to check and respond to emails and used templates for common responses. These practices improved his email communication and increased his productivity.

Rachel's Use of Email Management Tools Rachel, a marketing director, faced challenges with prioritizing emails. She started using SaneBox to filter important emails and Unroll.Me to manage her subscriptions. Rachel also set up filters to sort incoming messages and used the two-minute rule to handle quick tasks. These tools and strategies helped Rachel prioritize her emails and manage her inbox more effectively.

Mark's Email Boundaries Mark, a software developer, found that checking emails constantly disrupted his workflow. He set clear boundaries for email use by designating specific times to check his inbox and turning off notifications outside of these times. Mark also communicated his email boundaries to his team. These changes helped Mark maintain focus and improved his work-life balance.

Emily's Email Templates Emily, a customer service representative, spent a lot of time responding to similar inquiries. She created templates for common responses, which she customized as needed. Emily also used filters to sort incoming emails and prioritized her responses based on urgency. These practices saved her time and improved the efficiency of her email management.

Conclusion

Transforming your email management is essential for reducing stress and increasing productivity. By aiming for inbox zero, prioritizing effectively, communicating efficiently, using email management tools, setting email boundaries, creating templates, archiving and deleting regularly, and following the two-minute rule, you can take control of your inbox and enhance your overall efficiency. Implement these strategies to revolutionize the way you handle emails and achieve greater work-life balance.

Chapter 12: Morning Routines for Digital Productivity

The Sunrise Ritual

A student, seeking to start the day with clarity and purpose, asked the master, "How can I create a morning routine that enhances my productivity?"

The master took the student to a hilltop at dawn. They sat in silence, watching as the sun began to rise. The master then said, "Observe how the day begins."

The student watched as the darkness gradually gave way to light, the birds began to sing, and the world slowly came to life.

The master spoke, "Just as the sunrise unfolds naturally, so should your morning. Begin with stillness, then gently awaken your mind and body. Each step prepares you for the day ahead."

The student asked, "What steps should I take?"

The master replied, "Start with quiet reflection, nourish your body, move to awaken your energy, and set your intentions. This routine, like the sunrise, will bring light and productivity to your day."

The student understood and began each morning with a thoughtful routine, finding clarity and enhanced productivity throughout the day.

Introduction

THE WAY YOU START YOUR morning sets the tone for the rest of your day. A well-structured morning routine can enhance your digital productivity, boost your mood, and improve overall well-being. This chapter explores the importance of morning routines and provides practical tips to help you start your day with focus and intention.

Understanding the Power of Morning Routines

MORNING ROUTINES ARE a series of activities you perform at the start of your day to prepare yourself mentally, physically, and emotionally. Dr. Nikole Benders-Hadi, a psychiatrist, emphasizes that a consistent morning routine can reduce stress, increase productivity, and improve mental health. David Allen, the author of *Getting Things Done*, suggests that an effective morning routine can set the stage for a productive day by providing structure and clarity.

Expert Insights and Research

RESEARCH FROM THE *Journal of Applied Social Psychology* indicates that individuals who follow a structured morning routine experience higher levels of productivity and well-being. The study found that morning routines help create a sense of control and reduce the likelihood of procrastination.

Dr. John Ratey, author of *Spark: The Revolutionary New Science of Exercise and the Brain*, highlights the benefits of incorporating physical activity into your morning routine. Exercise has been shown to improve cognitive function, boost mood, and increase energy levels.

Practical Steps and Tips

1. START WITH A MINDFUL Moment Begin your morning with a few minutes of mindfulness or meditation. This practice helps center your mind, reduce stress, and set a positive tone for the day. Use apps like Headspace or Calm to guide your meditation sessions. Dr. Nikole Benders-Hadi recommends starting with just five minutes and gradually increasing the duration as you become more comfortable.

2. Hydrate Your Body After a night's sleep, your body is dehydrated. Drink a glass of water first thing in the morning to kickstart your metabolism and improve cognitive function. Nutritionist Lisa Drayer suggests adding a slice of lemon for a refreshing boost.

3. Engage in Physical Activity Incorporating exercise into your morning routine can enhance your physical and mental well-being. Whether it's a brisk walk, yoga, or a full workout, physical activity helps increase blood flow, improve mood, and boost energy levels. Dr. John Ratey's research shows that exercise stimulates the production of neurotransmitters that enhance brain function.

4. Eat a Nutritious Breakfast A balanced breakfast provides the energy and nutrients your body needs to function optimally. Choose foods rich in protein, healthy fats, and complex carbohydrates. Nutritionist Lisa Drayer recommends options like oatmeal with nuts and berries, a smoothie with spinach and protein powder, or whole-grain toast with avocado.

5. Plan Your Day Take a few minutes to review your tasks and set priorities for the day. Use a planner or digital app to organize your to-do list and allocate time for each task. David Allen suggests breaking down larger projects into smaller, manageable steps to prevent feeling overwhelmed.

6. Limit Screen Time Avoid immediately reaching for your phone or computer when you wake up. Instead, spend the first hour of your morning engaging in offline activities like reading, journaling, or stretching. This practice helps reduce digital overload and allows you to start your day with a clear mind.

7. Practice Gratitude Incorporate gratitude into your morning routine by listing three things you are thankful for. This practice can improve your mood, increase resilience, and enhance overall well-being. The *Journal of Positive Psychology* reports that practicing gratitude can lead to higher levels of happiness and life satisfaction.

Additional Tips for a Productive Morning Routine

1. ESTABLISH A CONSISTENT Wake-Up Time Waking up at the same time every day helps regulate your body's internal clock and improves sleep quality. Dr. Charles Czeisler from Harvard Medical School recommends maintaining a consistent sleep schedule even on weekends.

2. Prepare the Night Before Set yourself up for success by preparing for your morning routine the night before. Lay out your clothes, pack your bag, and prepare breakfast ingredients. This reduces decision fatigue and allows you to start your day smoothly.

3. Create a Calming Environment Set up a calming environment in your home to support your morning routine. Use soft lighting, play calming music, and keep your space tidy. A peaceful environment can help reduce stress and create a positive start to your day.

4. Use a Morning Playlist Create a playlist of your favorite uplifting songs to listen to as you go through your morning routine. Music can boost your mood, increase motivation, and make your routine more enjoyable.

5. Set Intentions for the Day Set positive intentions for your day by visualizing your goals and affirming your abilities. This practice can increase motivation and focus, helping you stay on track throughout the day.

Do's and Don'ts of Morning Routines

DO'S:

- **Do start with mindfulness**: Begin your morning with a few minutes of mindfulness or meditation to center your mind.

- **Do hydrate your body**: Drink a glass of water first thing in the morning to kickstart your metabolism.

- **Do engage in physical activity**: Incorporate exercise into your morning routine to boost energy levels and improve mood.

- **Do eat a nutritious breakfast**: Choose foods rich in protein, healthy fats, and complex carbohydrates.

- **Do plan your day**: Review your tasks and set priorities to organize your day effectively.

- **Do limit screen time**: Avoid reaching for your phone or computer immediately upon waking.

- **Do practice gratitude**: List three things you are thankful for to improve your mood and well-being.

• **Do establish a consistent wake-up time**: Maintain a regular sleep schedule to regulate your body's internal clock.

• **Do prepare the night before**: Set yourself up for success by preparing for your morning routine in advance.

• **Do create a calming environment**: Set up a peaceful space to support your morning routine.

• **Do use a morning playlist**: Listen to uplifting music to boost your mood and motivation.

• **Do set intentions for the day**: Visualize your goals and affirm your abilities to increase focus and motivation.

Don'ts:

• **Don't skip breakfast**: A nutritious breakfast is essential for providing the energy and nutrients your body needs.

• **Don't rush through your routine**: Take your time to go through each step mindfully and with intention.

• **Don't neglect hydration**: Staying hydrated is crucial for maintaining cognitive function and overall well-being.

• **Don't ignore physical activity**: Incorporating exercise into your morning routine can significantly enhance your productivity and mood.

• **Don't immediately reach for screens**: Allow yourself time to wake up fully and engage in offline activities before checking your phone or computer.

• **Don't overlook the power of gratitude**: Practicing gratitude can improve your mood and increase overall happiness.

- **Don't ignore preparation**: Preparing for your morning routine the night before can reduce decision fatigue and make your morning smoother.

- **Don't neglect a calming environment**: Creating a peaceful space can help reduce stress and create a positive start to your day.

- **Don't forget to set intentions**: Setting positive intentions can increase motivation and focus throughout the day.

FAQ: Morning Routines for Digital Productivity

Q: WHY ARE MORNING routines important for productivity? A: Morning routines help set a positive tone for the day, reduce stress, and increase productivity by providing structure and clarity. They create a sense of control and prepare you mentally, physically, and emotionally for the day ahead.

Q: How can I start a morning routine? A: Begin by incorporating simple activities such as mindfulness, hydration, and physical activity into your morning. Gradually add more steps like planning your day, practicing gratitude, and limiting screen time.

Q: How long should my morning routine be? A: The length of your morning routine depends on your schedule and preferences. Start with a few minutes for each activity and adjust as needed. Aim for a routine that you can consistently follow without feeling rushed.

Q: What are the benefits of practicing mindfulness in the morning? A: Mindfulness helps center your mind, reduce stress, and set a positive tone for the day. It improves focus, enhances emotional regulation, and increases overall well-being.

Q: How can I incorporate physical activity into my morning routine? A: Choose activities that you enjoy, such as walking, yoga, or a full workout. Schedule time for exercise in your morning routine and gradually increase the duration and intensity as you become more comfortable.

Q: What should I eat for breakfast to boost productivity? A: Choose a balanced breakfast that includes protein, healthy fats, and complex carbohydrates. Examples include oatmeal with nuts and berries, a smoothie with spinach and protein powder, or whole-grain toast with avocado.

Q: How can I limit screen time in the morning? A: Avoid immediately reaching for your phone or computer when you wake up. Instead, spend the first hour of your morning engaging in offline activities like reading, journaling, or stretching.

Q: What are some tips for creating a calming morning environment? A: Use soft lighting, play calming music, and keep your space tidy. A peaceful environment can help reduce stress and create a positive start to your day.

Q: How can I set intentions for the day? A: Visualize your goals and affirm your abilities. Set positive intentions by thinking about what you want to achieve and how you will approach your tasks with focus and motivation.

Q: What is the importance of gratitude in a morning routine? A: Practicing gratitude improves mood, increases resilience, and enhances overall well-being. Listing three things you are thankful for each morning can lead to higher levels of happiness and life satisfaction.

Case Studies and Examples

SOPHIA'S ENERGIZING Morning Routine Sophia, a software developer, struggled with feeling groggy and unmotivated in the mornings. She started incorporating mindfulness, hydration, and a short workout into her morning routine. Sophia also ate a nutritious breakfast and planned her day using a digital planner. These changes helped her feel more energized and focused throughout the day.

John's Screen-Free Start John, a graphic designer, found that checking his phone first thing in the morning increased his stress levels. He decided to create a screen-free morning routine that included journaling, stretching, and listening to music. John also practiced gratitude and set positive intentions for his day. This new routine helped him start his mornings with a clear mind and reduced stress.

Rachel's Consistent Wake-Up Time Rachel, a marketing manager, often felt tired and unproductive due to irregular sleep patterns. She established a consistent wake-up time and created a morning routine that included drinking water, practicing yoga, and planning her day. Rachel also prepared for her mornings the night before. These adjustments improved her sleep quality and overall productivity.

Mark's Gratitude Practice Mark, a college student, experienced anxiety and difficulty focusing in the mornings. He started incorporating gratitude into his morning routine by listing three things he was thankful for each day. Mark also engaged in mindfulness meditation and a short workout. These practices helped reduce his anxiety and increased his ability to concentrate on his studies.

Emily's Calming Environment Emily, a customer service representative, often felt rushed and stressed in the mornings. She created a calming environment by using soft lighting, playing relaxing music, and keeping her space tidy. Emily also drank water, practiced mindfulness, and set intentions for her day. These changes helped her start her mornings peacefully and improved her overall well-being.

Conclusion

A WELL-STRUCTURED MORNING routine is essential for enhancing digital productivity and overall well-being. By starting your day with mindfulness, hydration, physical activity, a nutritious breakfast, planning, and gratitude, you can set a positive tone for the rest of your day. Implement these strategies to create a morning routine that works for you and helps you achieve greater focus, motivation, and productivity.

Chapter 13: The Profound Effects of a Social Media Detox

The Quiet Lake

A novice, feeling overwhelmed by constant social media updates, asked the master, "How can I find peace and clarity when my mind is always buzzing with notifications?"

The master led the novice to a still lake and said, "Look into the water."

The novice saw their reflection clearly in the calm, undisturbed surface of the lake. The master then tossed a stone into the water, creating ripples that distorted the reflection.

The master explained, "The lake is your mind, and the stone is social media. When left undisturbed, the mind is clear and reflective. But constant disturbances create ripples, obscuring clarity."

The novice asked, "How can I keep my mind like the still lake?"

The master replied, "Withdraw from the constant influx. Allow the ripples to settle. Embrace moments of silence and reflection without the noise of social media."

The novice understood and began practicing regular social media detoxes, finding profound peace and clarity as their mind became like the quiet lake.

Introduction

SOCIAL MEDIA HAS BECOME a ubiquitous part of modern life, providing us with a way to connect, share, and consume information. However, excessive use of social media can lead to negative mental and emotional effects. This chapter explores the profound benefits of taking a break from social media and provides practical tips for implementing a social media detox.

Understanding Social Media Detox

A SOCIAL MEDIA DETOX involves taking a deliberate break from social media platforms to reduce stress, anxiety, and other negative effects associated with their use. Dr. Larry Rosen, a psychologist specializing in technology use, explains that periodic breaks from social media can significantly improve mental health and well-being.

Expert Insights and Research

RESEARCH FROM THE *Journal of Social and Clinical Psychology* indicates that reducing social media use can lead to significant improvements in mental health. The study found that participants who limited their social media use to 30 minutes per day experienced lower levels of anxiety, depression, and loneliness.

Sherry Turkle, a professor at MIT and author of *Reclaiming Conversation: The Power of Talk in a Digital Age*, highlights the importance of face-to-face interactions for building meaningful relationships. Turkle's research shows that excessive social media use can hinder these interactions and negatively impact our social connections.

Practical Steps and Tips

1. SET CLEAR GOALS for Your Detox Before starting a social media detox, identify your reasons for taking a break and set clear goals. Whether it's to reduce stress, improve productivity, or reconnect with loved ones, having a clear purpose will help you stay motivated throughout the detox.

2. Decide on the Duration Determine how long you want your social media detox to last. This could be a day, a week, a month, or longer. Choose a duration that feels achievable and aligns with your goals.

3. Inform Your Network Let your friends and followers know that you'll be taking a break from social media. This can help manage their expectations and provide a sense of accountability. Consider posting a message on your social media profiles explaining your decision.

4. Remove Social Media Apps Delete social media apps from your phone to reduce temptation. This simple step can make it easier to avoid mindless scrolling and stay committed to your detox. If you need to access certain platforms for work, consider using them only on your computer and setting specific times for use.

5. Find Alternative Activities Identify activities to fill the time you would typically spend on social media. This could include reading, exercising, spending time with family and friends, or pursuing hobbies. Engaging in meaningful activities can enhance your well-being and provide a sense of fulfillment.

6. Practice Mindfulness Incorporate mindfulness practices into your daily routine to help manage stress and stay present. Techniques such as meditation, deep breathing, and journaling can help you stay grounded and focused during your detox. Use apps like Headspace or Calm for guided mindfulness sessions.

7. Reflect on Your Experience At the end of your detox, take time to reflect on your experience. Consider the positive changes you noticed, such as improved mood, increased productivity, or stronger relationships. Use these insights to inform your future social media use and set boundaries to maintain a healthy balance.

Additional Tips for a Successful Social Media Detox

1. CREATE TECH-FREE Zones Designate specific areas in your home where social media and digital devices are not allowed. Common tech-free zones include the dining room, bedroom, and living room. This helps create physical boundaries and encourages more meaningful interactions.

2. Use Digital Well-Being Tools Many devices and apps offer digital well-being features that can help you manage your screen time. Use these tools to set limits on social media use, track your screen time, and receive reminders to take breaks.

3. Stay Connected Offline Make an effort to stay connected with friends and family through offline activities. Schedule regular meetups, phone calls, or video chats to maintain your social connections without relying on social media.

4. Keep a Journal Document your thoughts and feelings throughout your social media detox in a journal. This can help you process your experience and track your progress. Journaling can also serve as a valuable tool for self-reflection and personal growth.

5. Seek Support If you find it challenging to stay off social media, seek support from friends, family, or support groups. Sharing your goals and challenges with others can provide encouragement and accountability.

Do's and Don'ts of a Social Media Detox

DO'S:

- **Do set clear goals**: Identify your reasons for taking a break and set clear objectives.

- **Do decide on the duration**: Choose a realistic duration for your detox that aligns with your goals.

- **Do inform your network**: Let friends and followers know about your detox to manage expectations.

- **Do remove social media apps**: Delete apps from your phone to reduce temptation.

- **Do find alternative activities**: Engage in meaningful activities to fill the time you would spend on social media.

- **Do practice mindfulness**: Incorporate mindfulness techniques to stay present and manage stress.

- **Do reflect on your experience**: Take time to reflect on the positive changes you noticed during your detox.

- **Do create tech-free zones**: Designate areas in your home where digital devices are not allowed.

- **Do use digital well-being tools**: Utilize features that help you manage screen time and set limits.

- **Do stay connected offline**: Maintain social connections through offline activities and interactions.

- **Do keep a journal**: Document your thoughts and feelings to track your progress and reflect on your experience.

- **Do seek support**: Share your goals and challenges with others for encouragement and accountability.

Don'ts:

- **Don't go cold turkey**: Gradually reduce your social media use if needed, rather than quitting abruptly.

- **Don't ignore your goals**: Keep your objectives in mind to stay motivated throughout your detox.

- **Don't replace social media with other digital distractions**: Engage in offline activities that provide fulfillment.

- **Don't neglect mindfulness**: Practicing mindfulness can help you manage stress and stay present.

- **Don't isolate yourself**: Stay connected with friends and family through offline interactions.

- **Don't forget to reflect**: Reflecting on your experience can provide valuable insights for future social media use.

- **Don't be too hard on yourself**: If you slip up, acknowledge it and refocus on your goals without judgment.

- **Don't rely solely on willpower**: Use tools and strategies to support your detox and reduce temptation.

FAQ: Social Media Detox

Q: WHAT IS A SOCIAL media detox? A: A social media detox involves taking a deliberate break from social media platforms to reduce stress, anxiety, and other negative effects associated with their use.

Q: How long should a social media detox last? A: The duration of a social media detox can vary depending on your goals and preferences. It could be a day, a week, a month, or longer. Choose a duration that feels achievable and aligns with your objectives.

Q: What are the benefits of a social media detox? A: Benefits include reduced stress and anxiety, improved mood, increased productivity, stronger relationships, and a greater sense of well-being.

Q: How can I prepare for a social media detox? A: Set clear goals, decide on the duration, inform your network, remove social media apps from your phone, and identify alternative activities to fill your time.

Q: What should I do during a social media detox? A: Engage in meaningful offline activities, practice mindfulness, create tech-free zones, use digital well-being tools, stay connected with friends and family, and keep a journal to document your experience.

Q: How can I manage social media use after a detox? A: Reflect on your detox experience and set boundaries for future social media use. Limit your screen time, prioritize offline interactions, and use digital well-being tools to maintain a healthy balance.

Q: What if I find it challenging to stay off social media? A: Seek support from friends, family, or support groups. Share your goals and challenges with others for encouragement and accountability. Use tools and strategies to reduce temptation and stay committed to your detox.

Case Studies and Examples

SOPHIA'S WEEK-LONG Detox Sophia, a project manager, felt overwhelmed by the constant notifications and comparisons on social media. She decided to take a week-long social media detox to reduce stress and focus on her well-being. Sophia informed her friends about her break, deleted social media apps from her phone, and engaged in activities like hiking, reading, and cooking. By the end of the week, she noticed improved mood, increased productivity, and stronger connections with her family.

John's Digital Well-Being Tools John, a marketing executive, found that he was spending too much time on social media, affecting his work and personal life. He used digital well-being tools to set limits on his social media use and received reminders to take breaks. John also created tech-free zones in his home and scheduled regular meetups with friends. These changes helped him regain control over his social media use and improve his overall well-being.

Rachel's Mindfulness Practice Rachel, a college student, experienced anxiety and difficulty focusing due to excessive social media use. She incorporated mindfulness practices into her daily routine, such as meditation and journaling, to stay present and manage stress. Rachel also took a month-long social media detox and engaged in activities like painting and volunteering. These practices helped reduce her anxiety and increased her ability to concentrate on her studies.

Mark's Offline Connections Mark, a software developer, noticed that his social media use was affecting his relationships with friends and family. He decided to take a break from social media and focus on offline connections. Mark scheduled regular phone calls and meetups with loved ones, and participated in group activities like hiking and game nights. These efforts strengthened his relationships and provided a sense of fulfillment.

Emily's Reflective Detox Emily, a customer service representative, felt constantly stressed by the pressures of social media. She decided to take a two-week social media detox and reflect on her experience. Emily kept a journal to document her thoughts and feelings, practiced gratitude, and engaged in activities like gardening and yoga. By the end of the detox, she felt more relaxed, present, and connected to herself and her surroundings.

Conclusion

A SOCIAL MEDIA DETOX can have profound effects on your mental and emotional well-being. By setting clear goals, deciding on the duration, informing your network, removing social media apps, finding alternative activities, practicing mindfulness, and reflecting on your experience, you can successfully take a break from social media and reap the benefits. Implement these strategies to improve your mood, increase productivity, and enhance your overall well-being.

Chapter 14: Extreme Time-Blocking for Focus

T*he Stone Path*

A diligent student asked the master, "How can I achieve deeper focus and accomplish more with my time?"

The master pointed to a stone path leading through a garden and said, "Walk this path to the end without straying."

The student began, but soon noticed the beautiful flowers and interesting stones beside the path, getting distracted and wandering off. After a while, the student returned, having not reached the end.

The master said, "Now, walk again, but this time, place your feet only on the stones."

Focused on the stones, the student walked the path without distraction, reaching the end swiftly and efficiently.

The master explained, "Your time is like this path, and tasks are the stones. By focusing solely on the next stone, you avoid distractions and make steady progress. This is the essence of extreme time-blocking."

The student understood and began practicing extreme time-blocking, achieving greater focus and productivity by dedicating specific blocks of time to individual tasks.

Introduction

TIME-BLOCKING IS A powerful productivity technique that involves dividing your day into blocks of time, each dedicated to a specific task or activity. Extreme time-blocking takes this method to the next level by scheduling every minute of your day to maximize focus and efficiency. This chapter explores the principles of extreme time-blocking and provides practical strategies to help you organize your day and achieve more.

Understanding Extreme Time-Blocking

EXTREME TIME-BLOCKING involves meticulously planning your day by allocating specific time slots for each task, project, or activity. This technique helps reduce distractions, increase focus, and improve time management. Cal Newport, author of *Deep Work*, advocates for time-blocking as a way to achieve deep focus and produce high-quality work.

Expert Insights and Research

RESEARCH FROM THE *Journal of Applied Psychology* highlights the benefits of time management techniques like time-blocking. The study found that individuals who used time-blocking reported higher levels of productivity, reduced stress, and improved work-life balance.

Dr. Gloria Mark from the University of California, Irvine, emphasizes that time-blocking can help individuals manage their attention more effectively by minimizing multitasking and interruptions. Her research shows that focused work sessions can significantly enhance cognitive performance and overall productivity.

Practical Steps and Tips

1. PLAN YOUR DAY IN Advance Start by planning your day the night before or first thing in the morning. Outline your tasks and allocate specific time slots for each activity. Use a planner, digital calendar, or time-blocking app to organize your schedule. David Allen, author of *Getting Things Done*, suggests breaking down larger projects into smaller, manageable tasks to make time-blocking more effective.

2. Prioritize Your Tasks Identify your most important tasks (MITs) and schedule them during your peak productivity hours. These are the times of day when you are most focused and alert. Prioritizing your MITs ensures that you tackle your most critical work when you are at your best.

3. Set Clear Boundaries Establish clear boundaries around your time blocks to minimize interruptions. Communicate your schedule to colleagues, family, and friends, and let them know when you are not available. Use tools like Do Not Disturb mode on your devices to reduce distractions during focused work sessions.

4. Use the Pomodoro Technique Incorporate the Pomodoro Technique into your time-blocking schedule to maintain focus and prevent burnout. This method involves working for 25-minute intervals (Pomodoros) followed by short breaks. After completing four Pomodoros, take a longer break. Francesco Cirillo, the creator of the Pomodoro Technique, emphasizes that regular breaks help maintain energy levels and improve concentration.

5. Be Realistic with Your Schedule When time-blocking, be realistic about how long tasks will take and avoid overloading your schedule. Leave buffer time between tasks to account for unexpected interruptions or delays. Dr. Gloria Mark's research suggests that building flexibility into your schedule can help reduce stress and improve overall productivity.

6. Review and Adjust Your Schedule At the end of each day, review your schedule to assess what worked well and what didn't. Adjust your time blocks as needed to improve efficiency and accommodate any changes in priorities. Regularly reviewing and refining your schedule helps you stay on track and continuously improve your time management skills.

Additional Tips for Extreme Time-Blocking

1. USE COLOR-CODING Color-code your time blocks to differentiate between types of tasks and activities. For example, use one color for work-related tasks, another for personal activities, and a third for breaks. This visual distinction can help you quickly identify and manage your schedule.

2. Batch Similar Tasks Group similar tasks together and schedule them in the same time block. This approach, known as task batching, reduces the cognitive load associated with switching between different types of activities and improves efficiency.

3. Schedule Downtime Include downtime and self-care activities in your time-blocking schedule. Regular breaks, exercise, and relaxation are essential for maintaining overall well-being and preventing burnout. Dr. John Ratey's research highlights the importance of physical activity for cognitive function and mental health.

4. Track Your Progress Use a journal or digital tool to track your progress and monitor how well you adhere to your time blocks. Recording your accomplishments and identifying areas for improvement can help you stay motivated and make necessary adjustments.

5. Limit Time Spent on Email and Meetings Allocate specific time blocks for checking email and attending meetings. Avoid letting these activities consume your entire day by setting strict time limits. Use tools like Boomerang to schedule emails and focus on deep work during other time blocks.

6. Embrace Flexibility While extreme time-blocking provides structure, it's essential to remain flexible and adapt to changing circumstances. If a task takes longer than expected or an urgent issue arises, adjust your schedule accordingly. Flexibility ensures that you can accommodate unexpected events without compromising your overall productivity.

Do's and Don'ts of Extreme Time-Blocking

DO'S:

• **Do plan your day in advance**: Outline your tasks and allocate specific time slots for each activity.

• **Do prioritize your tasks**: Identify your most important tasks and schedule them during peak productivity hours.

• **Do set clear boundaries**: Communicate your schedule to minimize interruptions and reduce distractions.

• **Do use the Pomodoro Technique**: Incorporate regular breaks to maintain focus and prevent burnout.

• **Do be realistic with your schedule**: Allow buffer time between tasks and avoid overloading your schedule.

- **Do review and adjust your schedule**: Regularly assess and refine your time blocks to improve efficiency.

- **Do use color-coding**: Differentiate between types of tasks with color-coded time blocks.

- **Do batch similar tasks**: Group similar tasks together to reduce cognitive load and improve efficiency.

- **Do schedule downtime**: Include self-care activities and regular breaks to maintain well-being.

- **Do track your progress**: Monitor your adherence to time blocks and identify areas for improvement.

- **Do limit time spent on email and meetings**: Allocate specific time blocks for these activities and set strict time limits.

- **Do embrace flexibility**: Adapt to changing circumstances and adjust your schedule as needed.

Don'ts:

- **Don't neglect planning**: Failing to plan your day can lead to disorganization and reduced productivity.

- **Don't ignore priorities**: Ensure that your most important tasks are scheduled during your peak productivity hours.

- **Don't overlook boundaries**: Clear boundaries are essential for minimizing interruptions and staying focused.

- **Don't skip breaks**: Regular breaks are crucial for maintaining energy levels and preventing burnout.

- **Don't overestimate your capacity**: Be realistic about how long tasks will take and avoid overloading your schedule.

- **Don't forget to review your schedule**: Regularly assessing and refining your time blocks helps you stay on track.

- **Don't rely solely on willpower**: Use tools and strategies to support your time-blocking efforts and reduce temptation.

FAQ: Extreme Time-Blocking

Q: WHAT IS EXTREME time-blocking? A: Extreme time-blocking involves meticulously planning your day by allocating specific time slots for each task, project, or activity. This technique helps reduce distractions, increase focus, and improve time management.

Q: How can I start using extreme time-blocking? A: Begin by planning your day in advance, outlining your tasks, and allocating specific time slots for each activity. Use a planner, digital calendar, or time-blocking app to organize your schedule.

Q: What are the benefits of extreme time-blocking? A: Benefits include increased focus, reduced distractions, improved time management, higher productivity, and better work-life balance.

Q: How do I prioritize my tasks for time-blocking? A: Identify your most important tasks (MITs) and schedule them during your peak productivity hours. These are the times of day when you are most focused and alert.

Q: What is the Pomodoro Technique? A: The Pomodoro Technique involves working for 25-minute intervals (Pomodoros) followed by short breaks. After completing four Pomodoros, take a longer break. This method helps maintain focus and prevent burnout.

Q: How can I minimize interruptions during time-blocking? A: Set clear boundaries, communicate your schedule to others, and use tools like Do Not Disturb mode on your devices to reduce distractions during focused work sessions.

Q: How can I be realistic with my time-blocking schedule? A: Be realistic about how long tasks will take and avoid overloading your schedule. Leave buffer time between tasks to account for unexpected interruptions or delays.

Q: How can I track my progress with time-blocking? A: Use a journal or digital tool to track your progress and monitor how well you adhere to your time blocks. Recording your accomplishments and identifying areas for improvement can help you stay motivated and make necessary adjustments.

Q: What should I do if I need to adjust my schedule? A: While extreme time-blocking provides structure, it's essential to remain flexible and adapt to changing circumstances. If a task takes longer than expected or an urgent issue arises, adjust your schedule accordingly.

Case Studies and Examples

SOPHIA'S TIME-BLOCKING Transformation Sophia, a software developer, struggled with managing multiple projects and constant interruptions. She implemented extreme time-blocking by planning her day in advance and allocating specific time slots for each task. Sophia used the Pomodoro Technique to maintain focus and took regular breaks to recharge. These changes helped her stay organized, reduce stress, and improve her overall productivity.

John's Prioritized Schedule John, a marketing executive, found that he was frequently distracted by emails and meetings. He started prioritizing his most important tasks and scheduling them during his peak productivity hours. John also set clear boundaries with his colleagues and used Do Not Disturb mode to minimize interruptions. These practices allowed him to focus on high-priority work and achieve better results.

Rachel's Color-Coded Calendar Rachel, a graphic designer, felt overwhelmed by her workload and struggled to stay organized. She began using a color-coded calendar to differentiate between work tasks, personal activities, and breaks. Rachel also batched similar tasks together and scheduled downtime for self-care. These strategies helped her manage her time more effectively and maintain a healthy work-life balance.

Mark's Task Batching Mark, a financial analyst, often found it challenging to switch between different types of tasks. He started grouping similar tasks together and scheduling them in the same time block. Mark also used digital tools to track his progress and monitor his adherence to his schedule. These changes improved his efficiency and reduced the cognitive load associated with task switching.

Emily's Flexible Approach Emily, a project manager, realized that her rigid schedule was causing stress and burnout. She embraced a more flexible approach to time-blocking by allowing buffer time between tasks and adjusting her schedule as needed. Emily also included regular breaks and self-care activities in her schedule. These adjustments helped her maintain focus, reduce stress, and enhance her overall well-being.

Conclusion

EXTREME TIME-BLOCKING is a powerful technique for maximizing focus and productivity by meticulously planning your day and allocating specific time slots for each task. By planning your day in advance, prioritizing tasks, setting clear boundaries, using the Pomodoro Technique, being realistic with your schedule, and regularly reviewing and adjusting your time blocks, you can achieve greater efficiency and balance. Implement these strategies to take control of your time and accomplish more with less stress.

Chapter 15: Wearables: Your Wellness Allies

The Guiding Lantern

A curious student asked the sage, "How can I use modern technology to improve my health and wellness?"

The sage handed the student a lantern and said, "Carry this lantern with you and let it guide your steps."

As the student walked with the lantern, it illuminated the path ahead, revealing obstacles and safe passages. The student felt secure and aware, avoiding hazards and walking with confidence.

The sage explained, "This lantern is like a wearable device. It sheds light on your health, guiding you to make better choices. It tracks your steps, monitors your heart, and reminds you to rest, much like the lantern shows the way in darkness."

The student asked, "How can I use it wisely?"

The sage replied, "Let it inform you, but do not become dependent. Use its guidance to enhance your awareness and wellness, not to replace your inner knowing."

The student understood and began using wearables as allies in their wellness journey, finding improved health and mindfulness through the gentle guidance of their digital lanterns.

Introduction

WEARABLE TECHNOLOGY has revolutionized the way we approach health and wellness. From fitness trackers to smartwatches, these devices offer valuable insights into our physical activity, sleep patterns, and overall health. This chapter explores how wearables can become your wellness allies, helping you monitor and improve various aspects of your health.

Understanding Wearable Technology

WEARABLES ARE ELECTRONIC devices that can be worn on the body, often as accessories or clothing, to monitor and track various health metrics. Dr. Mitesh Patel, a leading researcher in digital health at the University of Pennsylvania, explains that wearables provide real-time data that can empower individuals to make informed decisions about their health.

Expert Insights and Research

RESEARCH FROM THE *Journal of Medical Internet Research* highlights the effectiveness of wearable technology in promoting physical activity and improving health outcomes. The study found that individuals who used wearables were more likely to engage in regular exercise and achieve their fitness goals.

Dr. John Jakicic, a professor of health and physical activity at the University of Pittsburgh, emphasizes that wearables can enhance motivation and accountability by providing immediate feedback on progress. His research shows that consistent use of wearables can lead to significant improvements in physical activity levels and overall health.

Practical Steps and Tips

1. CHOOSE THE RIGHT Wearable for Your Needs There are various types of wearables available, each offering different features and functionalities. Consider your specific health goals and preferences when choosing a wearable. Popular options include fitness trackers like Fitbit, smartwatches like the Apple Watch, and specialized devices like the Oura Ring and the Whoop band for sleep tracking.

2. Set Clear Goals Define clear and achievable health goals to guide your use of wearables. Whether it's increasing daily steps, improving sleep quality, or monitoring heart health, having specific goals will help you make the most of your wearable device. Dr. Mitesh Patel recommends setting SMART goals (Specific, Measurable, Achievable, Relevant, Time-bound) to ensure success.

3. Monitor Your Physical Activity Wearables can track various aspects of physical activity, including steps taken, distance covered, calories burned, and active minutes. Use this data to monitor your progress and make adjustments to your exercise routine as needed. Dr. John Jakicic's research suggests aiming for at least 150 minutes of moderate-intensity exercise per week for optimal health.

4. Track Your Sleep Patterns Many wearables offer sleep tracking features that monitor the duration and quality of your sleep. Use this data to identify patterns and make adjustments to improve your sleep hygiene. The National Sleep Foundation recommends aiming for 7-9 hours of sleep per night for adults.

5. Monitor Your Heart Rate Heart rate monitoring is a valuable feature of many wearables, providing insights into your cardiovascular health. Track your resting heart rate, heart rate variability, and workout intensity to optimize your fitness routine. The American Heart Association suggests using heart rate data to ensure you're exercising within your target heart rate zone.

6. Use Reminders and Notifications Take advantage of reminders and notifications from your wearable to stay on track with your health goals. Set reminders to move, hydrate, take breaks, and complete workouts. These prompts can help you maintain healthy habits throughout the day.

Additional Tips for Maximizing the Benefits of Wearables

1. SYNC WITH HEALTH Apps Many wearables can sync with health and fitness apps to provide a comprehensive view of your health data. Use apps like MyFitnessPal, Strava, and Apple Health to track your progress, set goals, and receive personalized recommendations.

2. Share Your Data with Healthcare Providers Consider sharing your wearable data with your healthcare provider to gain insights and receive personalized advice. Dr. Mitesh Patel's research highlights the potential for wearables to enhance patient care by providing continuous health monitoring and facilitating remote consultations.

3. Join Online Communities Many wearables offer access to online communities where you can connect with others who share similar health goals. Join these communities to receive support, share tips, and participate in challenges. Social support can enhance motivation and accountability.

4. Customize Your Settings Explore the settings and features of your wearable to customize it to your preferences. Adjust notifications, set personalized goals, and choose the metrics you want to track. Customization can enhance your user experience and make your wearable more effective.

5. Stay Consistent Consistency is key to achieving long-term health benefits with wearables. Make a habit of wearing your device daily and regularly reviewing your data. Dr. John Jakicic emphasizes that consistent use of wearables can lead to significant improvements in health outcomes over time.

Do's and Don'ts of Using Wearables

DO'S:

- **Do choose the right wearable**: Select a device that aligns with your specific health goals and preferences.

- **Do set clear goals**: Define achievable health goals to guide your use of wearables.

- **Do monitor your physical activity**: Track steps, distance, calories, and active minutes to optimize your exercise routine.

- **Do track your sleep patterns**: Use sleep tracking features to improve your sleep hygiene.

- **Do monitor your heart rate**: Track your heart rate to gain insights into your cardiovascular health.

- **Do use reminders and notifications**: Set reminders to maintain healthy habits throughout the day.

- **Do sync with health apps**: Integrate your wearable with health and fitness apps for a comprehensive view of your data.

- **Do share your data with healthcare providers**: Provide your healthcare provider with access to your data for personalized advice.

- **Do join online communities**: Connect with others who share similar health goals for support and motivation.

- **Do customize your settings**: Adjust your wearable's settings to suit your preferences.

- **Do stay consistent**: Wear your device daily and review your data regularly.

Don'ts:

- **Don't ignore your data**: Regularly review your wearable data to make informed decisions about your health.

- **Don't set unrealistic goals**: Ensure your health goals are achievable and aligned with your abilities.

- **Don't rely solely on your wearable**: Use wearables as a tool to complement, not replace, other healthy habits and practices.

- **Don't neglect other aspects of health**: Focus on overall well-being, including nutrition, mental health, and social connections.

- **Don't forget to charge your device**: Ensure your wearable is charged and functioning properly to maintain accurate tracking.

- **Don't ignore privacy settings**: Be aware of your wearable's privacy settings and control who has access to your data.

- **Don't become overly reliant on data**: Use your wearable data as a guide, but also listen to your body and intuition.

- **Don't neglect to update your device**: Keep your wearable's software up to date to benefit from the latest features and improvements.

FAQ: Wearables for Wellness

Q: WHAT ARE WEARABLES? A: Wearables are electronic devices worn on the body to monitor and track various health metrics, such as physical activity, sleep patterns, and heart rate.

Q: How can wearables improve my health? A: Wearables provide real-time data that can help you monitor your physical activity, sleep, and heart health. This information can guide your health decisions, increase motivation, and improve overall well-being.

Q: What should I consider when choosing a wearable? A: Consider your specific health goals and preferences. Popular options include fitness trackers like Fitbit, smartwatches like the Apple Watch, and specialized devices like the Oura Ring for sleep tracking.

Q: How do wearables track physical activity? A: Wearables use sensors to monitor steps taken, distance covered, calories burned, and active minutes. This data helps you track your progress and optimize your exercise routine.

Q: Can wearables track sleep patterns? A: Yes, many wearables offer sleep tracking features that monitor the duration and quality of your sleep. This data can help you identify patterns and make adjustments to improve your sleep hygiene.

Q: How can I use wearables to monitor my heart rate? A: Wearables with heart rate monitoring features track your resting heart rate, heart rate variability, and workout intensity. This data provides insights into your cardiovascular health and helps you optimize your fitness routine.

Q: What are the benefits of using reminders and notifications on wearables? A: Reminders and notifications help you stay on track with your health goals by prompting you to move, hydrate, take breaks, and complete workouts. These prompts can reinforce healthy habits and increase accountability.

Case Studies and Examples

SOPHIA'S FITNESS JOURNEY Sophia, a marketing manager, wanted to increase her physical activity and improve her overall fitness. She chose a Fitbit to track her steps, distance, and active minutes. Sophia set a goal of 10,000 steps per day and used the Fitbit app to monitor her progress. She also joined an online community of Fitbit users for support and motivation. Over several months, Sophia noticed significant improvements in her fitness levels and overall health.

John's Sleep Improvement John, a software developer, struggled with poor sleep quality and frequent waking during the night. He started using an Oura Ring to track his sleep patterns and identify areas for improvement. The Oura app provided insights into his sleep duration, sleep stages, and overall sleep quality. John made adjustments to his bedtime routine, such as reducing screen time before bed and creating a relaxing sleep environment. These changes helped him achieve more restful sleep and improved his daytime energy levels.

Rachel's Heart Health Monitoring Rachel, a teacher, wanted to monitor her heart health and ensure she was exercising within her target heart rate zone. She chose an Apple Watch with heart rate monitoring features to track her resting heart rate, heart rate variability, and workout intensity. Rachel used the Apple Health app to review her heart rate data and received personalized recommendations for her fitness routine. Regular monitoring helped Rachel optimize her workouts and maintain a healthy cardiovascular system.

Mark's Stress Management Mark, a financial analyst, experienced high levels of stress due to his demanding job. He started using a Garmin smartwatch with stress tracking features to monitor his stress levels throughout the day. The Garmin app provided insights into his stress patterns and offered guided breathing exercises to help manage stress. Mark incorporated these exercises into his daily routine and used the smartwatch's reminders to take regular breaks. These practices helped him reduce stress and improve his overall well-being.

Emily's Comprehensive Health Tracking Emily, a customer service representative, wanted to take a holistic approach to her health and wellness. She chose a Samsung Galaxy Watch to track her physical activity, sleep, heart rate, and stress levels. Emily set SMART goals for her fitness, sleep, and stress management, and used the Samsung Health app to monitor her progress. She also synced her watch with MyFitnessPal to track her nutrition and received personalized recommendations for her health journey. These efforts helped Emily achieve a balanced and healthy lifestyle.

Conclusion

WEARABLES ARE POWERFUL tools that can become your wellness allies by providing real-time data and insights into various aspects of your health. By choosing the right wearable, setting clear goals, monitoring physical activity, tracking sleep patterns, and using reminders and notifications, you can optimize your health and well-being. Implement these strategies to make the most of your wearable device and achieve your health goals.

Chapter 16: Decluttering Your Digital Life

T*he Clear Sky*

A disciple, feeling overwhelmed by digital clutter, asked the master, "How can I bring order to the chaos of my digital life?"

The master took the disciple to a hilltop on a foggy day. "Look at the sky," the master said.

The disciple could see nothing but thick fog, obscuring everything. The master then waited patiently with the disciple until the fog lifted, revealing a clear, blue sky.

The master explained, "Your digital life is like this sky. The clutter is the fog, obscuring clarity and peace. By removing unnecessary files, apps, and distractions, you clear the fog, revealing the clear sky within."

The disciple asked, "How can I clear the fog?"

The master replied, "Begin by identifying what is essential. Remove what does not serve your purpose. Organize and simplify. In this way, you will find clarity and peace."

The disciple understood and began decluttering their digital life, finding a sense of order and tranquility as the digital fog lifted, revealing the clear sky of simplicity.

Introduction

IN TODAY'S DIGITAL age, our devices are filled with an overwhelming amount of information and media. Digital clutter can lead to stress, decreased productivity, and difficulty finding important files. This chapter explores strategies for decluttering your digital life, simplifying your digital environment, and enhancing your overall well-being.

Understanding Digital Clutter

DIGITAL CLUTTER REFERS to the accumulation of unnecessary files, apps, emails, and other digital content that can overwhelm and distract us. Dr. Cal Newport, author of *Digital Minimalism*, explains that decluttering your digital life can lead to increased focus, reduced stress, and improved productivity.

Expert Insights and Research

RESEARCH FROM THE *Journal of Environmental Psychology* highlights the impact of digital clutter on mental health and productivity. The study found that individuals who decluttered their digital environment experienced lower stress levels and improved concentration.

Marie Kondo, author of *The Life-Changing Magic of Tidying Up*, emphasizes the importance of decluttering not just physical spaces but also digital spaces. Her KonMari method, which involves keeping only items that "spark joy," can be adapted to digital decluttering.

Practical Steps and Tips

1. ORGANIZE YOUR FILES and Folders Start by organizing your files and folders. Create a logical folder structure that makes it easy to find and access important documents. Use descriptive file names and categorize files by type, date, or project. Regularly review and clean out old or unnecessary files.

2. Clean Up Your Desktop A cluttered desktop can be distracting and hinder productivity. Remove unnecessary icons and files from your desktop and organize the remaining items into folders. Consider using a minimalist wallpaper to create a clean and calming workspace.

3. Unsubscribe from Unwanted Emails An overflowing inbox can be a significant source of digital clutter. Unsubscribe from newsletters, promotions, and other emails that you no longer find useful. Use tools like Unroll.Me to manage your subscriptions and reduce inbox clutter.

4. Delete Unused Apps Take stock of the apps on your devices and delete those that you no longer use. This frees up storage space and reduces distractions. Regularly review your apps and keep only those that add value to your digital life.

5. Organize Your Photos and Videos Digital photos and videos can quickly accumulate and take up significant storage space. Organize your media files into folders by date or event, and delete duplicates or low-quality images. Consider using cloud storage solutions like Google Photos or iCloud to back up and manage your media.

6. Clear Your Browser and Cache Regularly clear your browser history, cache, and cookies to improve performance and protect your privacy. Use bookmarks to save important websites and organize them into folders for easy access. Consider using browser extensions like Pocket or Evernote to save and organize web content.

Additional Tips for Decluttering Your Digital Life

1. SET DIGITAL BOUNDARIES Establish boundaries for your digital devices to prevent them from taking over your life. Set specific times for checking emails and social media, and designate tech-free zones in your home. Dr. Cal Newport recommends practicing digital minimalism by being intentional about your technology use.

2. Use Digital Tools for Organization Leverage digital tools and apps to help you stay organized and manage your digital clutter. Tools like Evernote, Trello, and Todoist can help you organize notes, tasks, and projects. Use cloud storage services like Google Drive or Dropbox to store and share files.

3. Automate Routine Tasks Automate repetitive tasks to save time and reduce digital clutter. Use tools like IFTTT (If This Then That) or Zapier to create automated workflows for tasks like saving email attachments, backing up files, or posting to social media.

4. Regularly Review and Update Your Digital Environment Set aside time each month to review and update your digital environment. Delete unnecessary files, update software and apps, and reorganize your digital workspace. Regular maintenance helps prevent digital clutter from accumulating and keeps your devices running smoothly.

5. Practice Mindful Technology Use Be mindful of how you use technology and the impact it has on your well-being. Take regular breaks from screens, practice digital detoxes, and focus on using technology in ways that enhance your life. Marie Kondo's principle of keeping only what "sparks joy" can be applied to your digital life as well.

Do's and Don'ts of Decluttering Your Digital Life
DO'S:

• **Do organize your files and folders**: Create a logical folder structure and use descriptive file names.

• **Do clean up your desktop**: Remove unnecessary icons and organize remaining items into folders.

• **Do unsubscribe from unwanted emails**: Use tools like Unroll.Me to manage subscriptions and reduce inbox clutter.

• **Do delete unused apps**: Regularly review and delete apps that you no longer use.

• **Do organize your photos and videos**: Categorize media files and delete duplicates or low-quality images.

• **Do clear your browser and cache**: Regularly clear your browser history, cache, and cookies for better performance.

• **Do set digital boundaries**: Establish specific times for checking emails and social media, and designate tech-free zones.

• **Do use digital tools for organization**: Leverage apps like Evernote, Trello, and Todoist to stay organized.

• **Do automate routine tasks**: Use tools like IFTTT or Zapier to create automated workflows.

• **Do regularly review and update your digital environment**: Set aside time each month for digital maintenance.

• **Do practice mindful technology use**: Be intentional about your technology use and focus on what enhances your life.

Don'ts:

• **Don't let files accumulate**: Regularly review and clean out old or unnecessary files.

• **Don't neglect your desktop**: Keep your desktop organized to reduce distractions.

• **Don't ignore your inbox**: Manage your email subscriptions to prevent inbox overload.

• **Don't hoard apps**: Delete apps that you no longer use to free up storage space.

• **Don't forget to organize your media**: Regularly review and categorize your photos and videos.

• **Don't overlook browser maintenance**: Clear your browser history, cache, and cookies regularly.

• **Don't ignore digital boundaries**: Set boundaries to prevent digital devices from taking over your life.

• **Don't rely solely on memory**: Use digital tools to stay organized and manage your digital clutter.

• **Don't waste time on repetitive tasks**: Automate routine tasks to save time and reduce clutter.

• **Don't neglect regular maintenance**: Regularly review and update your digital environment to prevent clutter.

- **Don't be mindless with technology**: Be mindful of your technology use and its impact on your well-being.

FAQ: Decluttering Your Digital Life

Q: WHAT IS DIGITAL clutter? A: Digital clutter refers to the accumulation of unnecessary files, apps, emails, and other digital content that can overwhelm and distract us.

Q: How can I organize my files and folders? A: Create a logical folder structure and use descriptive file names. Categorize files by type, date, or project, and regularly review and clean out old or unnecessary files.

Q: What are some tools for managing email subscriptions? A: Tools like Unroll.Me can help you manage your email subscriptions and reduce inbox clutter by allowing you to easily unsubscribe from unwanted emails.

Q: How often should I review and update my digital environment? A: Set aside time each month to review and update your digital environment. Regular maintenance helps prevent digital clutter from accumulating and keeps your devices running smoothly.

Q: What are some digital tools for organization? A: Apps like Evernote, Trello, and Todoist can help you organize notes, tasks, and projects. Use cloud storage services like Google Drive or Dropbox to store and share files.

Q: How can I practice mindful technology use? A: Be intentional about how you use technology and focus on what enhances your life. Take regular breaks from screens, practice digital detoxes, and use technology in ways that support your well-being.

Q: What is the KonMari method for digital decluttering? A: The KonMari method, developed by Marie Kondo, involves keeping only items that "spark joy." This principle can be applied to digital decluttering by keeping only the digital content that adds value to your life.

Case Studies and Examples

SOPHIA'S ORGANIZED Workspace Sophia, a project manager, felt overwhelmed by the clutter on her desktop and in her digital files. She started by organizing her files and folders, creating a logical structure that made it easy to find important documents.

Sophia also cleaned up her desktop, removing unnecessary icons and organizing the remaining items into folders. These changes helped her feel more in control of her digital environment and improved her productivity.

John's Email Overhaul John, a marketing executive, struggled with an overflowing inbox. He used Unroll.Me to manage his email subscriptions and unsubscribe from newsletters and promotions that he no longer found useful. John also set specific times for checking emails and created folders to categorize important messages. These strategies helped him reduce inbox clutter and manage his emails more effectively.

Rachel's App Detox Rachel, a graphic designer, noticed that her phone was filled with apps that she rarely used. She decided to declutter her device by deleting unused apps and organizing the remaining ones into folders. Rachel also reviewed her apps regularly to ensure that they added value to her digital life. These changes helped her reduce distractions and free up storage space.

Mark's Media Organization Mark, a college student, had thousands of photos and videos on his devices, making it difficult to find specific media files. He organized his photos and videos into folders by date and event, and deleted duplicates or low-quality images. Mark also used Google Photos to back up and manage his media files. These efforts helped him keep his media organized and easily accessible.

Emily's Digital Maintenance Routine Emily, a customer service representative, wanted to keep her digital environment organized and clutter-free. She set aside time each month to review and update her digital files, apps, and browser. Emily also used digital tools like Trello and Dropbox to stay organized and manage her projects. Regular maintenance helped her prevent digital clutter from accumulating and improved her overall efficiency.

Conclusion

DECLUTTERING YOUR DIGITAL life is essential for reducing stress, improving productivity, and enhancing overall well-being. By organizing your files and folders, cleaning up your desktop, managing email subscriptions, deleting unused apps, organizing media files, and practicing mindful technology use, you can create a simplified and efficient digital environment. Implement these strategies to take control of your digital life and enjoy the benefits of a clutter-free digital space.

Chapter 17: Stress Relief Through Digital Tools

The Soothing Melody

A weary seeker, burdened by stress, approached the sage and asked, "How can I find relief from my stress using digital tools?"

The sage took the seeker to a quiet grove and handed them a flute. "Play a single note," the sage instructed.

The seeker played a note, and the sound was clear and soothing, resonating through the grove. The sage then said, "Continue playing, letting the melody flow."

As the seeker played, the melody brought a sense of calm and relaxation. The sage explained, "The flute, like digital tools, can bring peace and relief when used with intention. Let the tools guide you to calm, just as the melody soothes your spirit."

The seeker asked, "Which tools should I use?"

The sage replied, "Choose tools that resonate with you—meditation apps, calming music, or guided breathing exercises. Use them mindfully to create your own melody of peace."

The seeker understood and began using digital tools for stress relief, finding that the mindful use of technology brought harmony and calm into their life, much like the soothing melody of the flute.

Introduction

STRESS IS A COMMON challenge in today's fast-paced digital world. Fortunately, technology can also provide solutions to help manage and alleviate stress. This chapter explores various digital tools and apps designed to reduce stress, promote relaxation, and improve mental well-being.

Understanding Digital Stress Relief Tools

DIGITAL STRESS RELIEF tools include apps and devices that offer relaxation techniques, guided meditations, breathing exercises, and other methods to help manage stress. Dr. Judson Brewer, a psychiatrist and neuroscientist at Brown University, explains that these tools can provide accessible and effective ways to reduce stress and improve mental health.

Expert Insights and Research

RESEARCH FROM THE *Journal of Medical Internet Research* indicates that digital interventions for stress management, such as mindfulness apps and virtual reality relaxation programs, can significantly reduce stress levels and improve overall well-being. The study found that individuals who used digital stress relief tools experienced lower anxiety and greater emotional resilience.

Dr. Emma Seppälä, author of *The Happiness Track*, highlights the benefits of mindfulness and relaxation techniques in reducing stress. Her research shows that practices like meditation and deep breathing can activate the body's relaxation response and decrease stress hormones.

Practical Steps and Tips

1. USE MINDFULNESS Apps Mindfulness apps, such as Headspace and Calm, offer guided meditations, breathing exercises, and relaxation techniques to help manage stress. These apps provide structured programs and short sessions that can fit into your daily routine. Dr. Judson Brewer's research emphasizes the effectiveness of mindfulness practices in reducing stress and improving emotional well-being.

2. Practice Breathing Exercises Breathing exercises can quickly reduce stress and promote relaxation. Apps like Breathe2Relax and Prana Breath guide you through various breathing techniques, such as diaphragmatic breathing and box breathing. Regular practice can help you manage stress more effectively.

3. Explore Virtual Reality (VR) Relaxation Virtual reality (VR) relaxation apps, such as Nature Treks VR and Guided

Meditation VR, offer immersive experiences that transport you to calming environments. These apps use VR technology to create a sense of presence and relaxation, making them effective tools for stress relief.

4. Use Journaling Apps Journaling is a powerful tool for managing stress and processing emotions. Digital journaling apps like Day One and Journey provide a convenient way to document your thoughts and feelings. Regular journaling can help you gain insights into your stressors and develop coping strategies.

5. Try Digital Therapy and Counseling Online therapy and counseling services, such as BetterHelp and Talkspace, offer convenient access to mental health professionals. These platforms provide video sessions, messaging, and other forms of support to help you manage stress and address mental health concerns.

Additional Tips for Using Digital Stress Relief Tools

1. SET REGULAR REMINDERS Use reminders to prompt you to practice stress relief techniques throughout the day. Many apps offer customizable notifications to help you stay consistent with your mindfulness, breathing exercises, or journaling.

2. Track Your Progress Many stress relief apps include features for tracking your progress over time. Monitoring your improvements can provide motivation and help you identify which techniques are most effective for you.

3. Create a Relaxing Digital Environment Optimize your digital environment by using calming wallpapers, soothing sounds, and low-brightness settings. Creating a relaxing digital space can enhance the effectiveness of your stress relief practices.

4. Combine Digital Tools with Offline Practices While digital tools are beneficial, it's also important to incorporate offline stress relief practices, such as physical exercise, spending time in nature, and connecting with loved ones. Combining digital and offline methods can provide a comprehensive approach to stress management.

5. Customize Your Experience Many apps and tools offer customization options to tailor the experience to your preferences. Experiment with different techniques, durations, and settings to find what works best for you.

Do's and Don'ts of Using Digital Stress Relief Tools

DO'S:

- **Do use mindfulness apps**: Incorporate guided meditations and relaxation techniques into your daily routine.

- **Do practice breathing exercises**: Use apps to guide you through effective breathing techniques for stress relief.

- **Do explore VR relaxation**: Try virtual reality apps for immersive and calming experiences.

- **Do use journaling apps**: Document your thoughts and feelings to process emotions and manage stress.

- **Do try digital therapy**: Access online therapy and counseling services for professional support.

- **Do set regular reminders**: Use notifications to stay consistent with your stress relief practices.

- **Do track your progress**: Monitor your improvements to stay motivated and identify effective techniques.

- **Do create a relaxing digital environment**: Use calming wallpapers, sounds, and settings to enhance relaxation.

- **Do combine digital and offline practices**: Integrate both methods for a comprehensive approach to stress management.

- **Do customize your experience**: Tailor apps and tools to your preferences for maximum effectiveness.

Don'ts:

- **Don't ignore stress signals**: Pay attention to your body's stress signals and take proactive steps to manage them.

- **Don't rely solely on digital tools**: Incorporate offline practices for a balanced approach to stress relief.

- **Don't neglect regular practice**: Consistency is key to experiencing the benefits of stress relief techniques.

- **Don't skip professional help**: Seek support from mental health professionals if needed.

- **Don't overlook customization**: Experiment with different techniques and settings to find what works best for you.

- **Don't ignore your progress**: Regularly track your improvements to stay motivated and informed.

- **Don't let digital tools become stressors**: Use apps and tools mindfully to enhance relaxation, not add to your stress.

FAQ: Digital Tools for Stress Relief

Q: WHAT ARE DIGITAL stress relief tools? A: Digital stress relief tools include apps and devices that offer relaxation techniques, guided meditations, breathing exercises, and other methods to help manage stress and improve mental well-being.

Q: How can mindfulness apps help with stress relief? A: Mindfulness apps, such as Headspace and Calm, provide guided meditations, breathing exercises, and relaxation techniques that can help reduce stress and improve emotional well-being.

Q: What are some effective breathing exercises for stress relief? A: Effective breathing exercises include diaphragmatic breathing, box breathing, and alternate nostril breathing. Apps like Breathe2Relax and Prana Breath can guide you through these techniques.

Q: How does virtual reality (VR) relaxation work? A: VR relaxation apps use virtual reality technology to create immersive experiences that transport you to calming environments. These apps can help reduce stress and promote relaxation by creating a sense of presence and tranquility.

Q: What are the benefits of digital journaling for stress relief? A: Digital journaling allows you to document your thoughts and feelings, process emotions, and gain insights into your stressors. Regular journaling can help you develop coping strategies and improve mental well-being.

Q: How can online therapy and counseling services help with stress management? A: Online therapy and counseling services, such as BetterHelp and Talkspace, provide convenient access to mental health professionals who can offer support and guidance for managing stress and addressing mental health concerns.

Q: How can I stay consistent with my stress relief practices? A: Set regular reminders and notifications to prompt you to practice stress relief techniques throughout the day. Use app features to track your progress and stay motivated.

Case Studies and Examples

SOPHIA'S MINDFULNESS Practice Sophia, a marketing manager, often felt overwhelmed by her workload and experienced high levels of stress. She started using the Headspace app to practice guided meditations and breathing exercises. Sophia set reminders to meditate for 10 minutes each morning and evening. Over time, she noticed a significant reduction in her stress levels and an improvement in her overall well-being.

John's VR Relaxation John, a software developer, struggled with anxiety and found it challenging to relax after a long day at work. He began using the Nature Treks VR app to immerse himself in calming virtual environments. John spent 20 minutes each evening exploring virtual beaches, forests, and underwater scenes. These VR experiences helped him unwind, reduce his anxiety, and improve his sleep quality.

Rachel's Journaling Routine Rachel, a teacher, experienced stress and emotional exhaustion from her demanding job. She started using the Day One app to document her thoughts and feelings. Rachel set aside 15 minutes each night to journal about her day, express gratitude, and reflect on her experiences. Regular journaling helped her process her emotions, gain clarity, and develop coping strategies.

Mark's Breathing Exercises Mark, a financial analyst, faced high-pressure situations at work that often led to stress and tension. He began using the Breathe2Relax app to practice diaphragmatic breathing exercises. Mark set reminders to take five-minute breathing breaks throughout the day. These exercises helped him stay calm, focused, and better manage stress.

Emily's Digital Therapy Emily, a customer service representative, struggled with chronic stress and anxiety. She signed up for online therapy through BetterHelp and had regular video sessions with a licensed therapist. Emily also used the BetterHelp app to message her therapist between sessions and track her progress. Access to professional support helped Emily develop effective stress management techniques and improve her mental well-being.

Conclusion

DIGITAL TOOLS OFFER powerful solutions for managing stress and promoting relaxation. By incorporating mindfulness apps, breathing exercises, VR relaxation, journaling, and online therapy into your routine, you can effectively reduce stress and improve your overall mental health. Implement these strategies to take control of your stress and enhance your well-being in the digital age.

Chapter 18: Harmonizing Screen and Offline Time

The Balance of Day and Night

A devoted student, struggling to balance screen time with offline life, asked the master, "How can I find harmony between my digital world and the real world?"

The master led the student to a quiet valley at dusk. "Observe the transition from day to night," the master said.

As the sun set and the stars began to appear, the valley transformed from the bright activity of day to the calm stillness of night. The master spoke, "Just as day transitions to night, you must balance your screen time with moments of stillness and connection to the real world."

The student asked, "How can I achieve this balance?"

The master replied, "Set boundaries for your screen time, just as day has its boundaries with night. Engage fully with the world during daylight hours, then embrace the calm of the night. Find your rhythm between activity and rest."

The student understood and began harmonizing screen and offline time, creating a balanced rhythm that brought peace and fulfillment to both their digital and real-world experiences.

Introduction

IN OUR DIGITAL AGE, balancing screen time with offline activities is crucial for maintaining overall well-being. Excessive screen time can lead to physical strain, mental fatigue, and reduced social interactions. This chapter explores strategies for harmonizing screen and offline time to enhance your health, productivity, and happiness.

Understanding the Balance

HARMONIZING SCREEN and offline time involves creating a balanced routine that incorporates both digital and non-digital activities. Dr. Larry Rosen, a psychologist and expert in technology use, emphasizes the importance of mindful technology use to prevent digital overload and promote a healthier lifestyle.

Expert Insights and Research

RESEARCH FROM THE *American Journal of Preventive Medicine* highlights the negative effects of excessive screen time on physical and mental health. The study found that individuals who spent more time on screens experienced higher levels of anxiety, depression, and physical discomfort.

Sherry Turkle, a professor at MIT and author of *Reclaiming Conversation: The Power of Talk in a Digital Age*, stresses the importance of face-to-face interactions for building meaningful relationships. Her research shows that balancing screen time with offline activities can improve social connections and overall well-being.

Practical Steps and Tips

1. SET SCREEN TIME Limits Establishing screen time limits can help you manage your digital use and prevent overexposure. Use built-in screen time management tools on your devices to set daily limits for specific apps and activities. Dr. Larry Rosen recommends setting specific times for digital activities and sticking to them to create a balanced routine.

2. Schedule Offline Activities Incorporate offline activities into your daily schedule to ensure a balanced mix of digital and non-digital time. Activities like reading, exercising, cooking, and spending time outdoors can provide a refreshing break from screens and enhance your overall well-being.

3. Create Tech-Free Zones Designate specific areas in your home where digital devices are not allowed. Common tech-free zones include the dining room, bedroom, and living room. Creating these spaces encourages more face-to-face interactions and reduces digital distractions.

4. Practice Mindful Technology Use Be intentional about how and when you use technology. Avoid mindlessly scrolling through social media or checking emails out of habit. Instead, focus on using technology for purposeful activities that add value to your life. Dr. Larry Rosen suggests taking regular breaks from screens to rest your eyes and mind.

5. Engage in Physical Activities Physical activities are essential for maintaining physical and mental health. Schedule regular exercise sessions, whether it's a morning jog, yoga class, or evening walk. Physical activities help reduce the negative effects of prolonged screen time and improve overall well-being.

Additional Tips for Harmonizing Screen and Offline Time

1. IMPLEMENT THE 20-20-20 Rule To prevent eye strain from prolonged screen use, follow the 20-20-20 rule: every 20 minutes, look at something 20 feet away for at least 20 seconds. This practice helps relax your eye muscles and reduce digital eye strain.

2. Set Digital Boundaries Establish clear boundaries for digital device use, such as no screens during meals or after a certain time in the evening. Communicate these boundaries to family members and colleagues to create a supportive environment.

3. Plan Digital Detox Periods Schedule regular digital detox periods where you completely disconnect from digital devices. This could be for a few hours, a day, or an entire weekend. Use this time to engage in offline activities, connect with loved ones, and recharge.

4. Use Technology to Support Offline Activities Leverage technology to enhance your offline experiences. For example, use fitness apps to track your workouts, cooking apps to explore new recipes, or meditation apps to guide your mindfulness practice. Combining digital and offline activities can create a balanced and fulfilling routine.

5. Foster In-Person Connections Make an effort to nurture in-person relationships by scheduling regular meetups with friends and family. Face-to-face interactions are crucial for building meaningful connections and maintaining social well-being.

Do's and Don'ts of Harmonizing Screen and Offline Time

DO'S:

- **Do set screen time limits**: Use built-in tools to manage your screen time and create a balanced routine.

- **Do schedule offline activities**: Incorporate non-digital activities into your daily schedule to ensure a healthy balance.

- **Do create tech-free zones**: Designate areas in your home where digital devices are not allowed.

- **Do practice mindful technology use**: Be intentional about your digital use and focus on purposeful activities.

- **Do engage in physical activities**: Schedule regular exercise sessions to maintain physical and mental health.

- **Do implement the 20-20-20 rule**: Take regular breaks to rest your eyes and reduce digital eye strain.

- **Do set digital boundaries**: Establish clear boundaries for digital device use and communicate them to others.

- **Do plan digital detox periods**: Schedule regular breaks from digital devices to recharge and reconnect.

- **Do use technology to support offline activities**: Leverage digital tools to enhance your offline experiences.

- **Do foster in-person connections**: Make an effort to nurture face-to-face relationships with friends and family.

Don'ts:

- **Don't ignore screen time limits**: Adhering to set limits is crucial for maintaining a balanced routine.

- **Don't neglect offline activities**: Ensure a healthy mix of digital and non-digital time in your daily schedule.

- **Don't let digital devices dominate your space**: Create tech-free zones to reduce digital distractions.

- **Don't use technology mindlessly**: Be intentional about your digital use and avoid mindless scrolling.

- **Don't skip physical activities**: Regular exercise is essential for counteracting the effects of prolonged screen time.

- **Don't overlook eye strain prevention**: Follow the 20-20-20 rule to reduce digital eye strain.

- **Don't ignore digital boundaries**: Establishing and maintaining boundaries is crucial for a balanced lifestyle.

- **Don't avoid digital detox periods**: Regular breaks from digital devices are essential for mental and emotional well-being.

- **Don't rely solely on technology**: Combine digital and offline activities for a fulfilling routine.

- **Don't neglect in-person relationships**: Face-to-face interactions are vital for social well-being.

FAQ: Harmonizing Screen and Offline Time

Q: WHAT IS THE IMPORTANCE of harmonizing screen and offline time? A: Balancing screen time with offline activities is crucial for maintaining physical, mental, and social well-being. Excessive screen time can lead to physical strain, mental fatigue, and reduced social interactions.

Q: How can I set screen time limits? A: Use built-in screen time management tools on your devices to set daily limits for specific apps and activities. Stick to these limits to create a balanced routine.

Q: What are some offline activities I can incorporate into my routine? A: Offline activities include reading, exercising, cooking, spending time outdoors, and engaging in hobbies. These activities provide a refreshing break from screens and enhance overall well-being.

Q: How can I create tech-free zones in my home? A: Designate specific areas where digital devices are not allowed, such as the dining room, bedroom, and living room. This encourages face-to-face interactions and reduces digital distractions.

Q: What is mindful technology use? A: Mindful technology use involves being intentional about how and when you use digital devices. Focus on purposeful activities and avoid mindless scrolling or checking emails out of habit.

Q: What is the 20-20-20 rule? A: The 20-20-20 rule is a practice to prevent eye strain from prolonged screen use. Every 20 minutes, look at something 20 feet away for at least 20 seconds to relax your eye muscles.

Q: How can I plan a digital detox period? A: Schedule regular periods where you completely disconnect from digital devices. Use this time to engage in offline activities, connect with loved ones, and recharge.

Q: How can technology support offline activities? A: Leverage digital tools to enhance your offline experiences, such as using fitness apps to track workouts, cooking apps to explore new recipes, or meditation apps to guide mindfulness practice.

Case Studies and Examples

SOPHIA'S BALANCED ROUTINE Sophia, a project manager, felt overwhelmed by constant screen time and digital distractions. She started setting screen time limits using her phone's built-in tools and scheduled daily offline activities like reading and exercising. Sophia also created tech-free zones in her home and practiced mindful technology use. These changes helped her achieve a balanced routine and improved her overall well-being.

John's Digital Detox John, a marketing executive, struggled with digital overload and mental fatigue. He decided to schedule regular digital detox periods where he completely disconnected from his devices. During these times, John engaged in activities like hiking, cooking, and spending time with friends. The digital detoxes helped him recharge and improved his mental clarity and focus.

Rachel's Tech-Free Zones Rachel, a teacher, noticed that her family's screen time was interfering with their quality time together. She designated the dining room and living room as tech-free zones, encouraging face-to-face interactions during meals and family time. Rachel also set digital boundaries for screen use in the evening. These changes fostered stronger family connections and reduced digital distractions.

Mark's Mindful Technology Use Mark, a software developer, found himself mindlessly scrolling through social media during breaks. He started practicing mindful technology use by setting specific times for checking emails and social media. Mark also incorporated physical activities into his routine, such as morning runs and evening yoga sessions. These practices helped him stay focused and balanced his screen and offline time.

Emily's Digital Well-Being Tools Emily, a customer service representative, wanted to harmonize her screen and offline time. She used digital well-being tools on her devices to track and limit her screen time. Emily also scheduled regular offline activities like gardening, painting, and spending time with friends. These efforts helped her create a balanced routine and improved her overall happiness and well-being.

Conclusion

HARMONIZING SCREEN and offline time is essential for maintaining overall well-being in the digital age. By setting screen time limits, scheduling offline activities, creating tech-free zones, practicing mindful technology use, and engaging in physical activities, you can achieve a balanced routine that enhances your health, productivity, and happiness. Implement these strategies to take control of your digital life and enjoy the benefits of a harmonious balance between screen and offline time.

Chapter 19: Mastering Do Not Disturb Mode

The Silent Bell

A disciple, constantly interrupted by notifications, asked the sage, "How can I find uninterrupted focus amidst the noise of alerts and messages?"

The sage took the disciple to a tranquil temple where a bell hung silently. The sage struck the bell once, and the sound resonated through the temple, then faded into silence.

The sage explained, "The bell's sound is like your notifications—disruptive yet temporary. Now, let the bell remain silent."

The disciple observed the stillness and peace that followed. The sage said, "Master the silence. Use the Do Not Disturb mode like this silent bell, allowing your mind to remain undisturbed and focused."

The disciple asked, "When should I activate this mode?"

The sage replied, "During moments of deep focus, rest, and reflection. Set clear boundaries for your work and rest, and let the silence guide you."

The disciple understood and began using Do Not Disturb mode mindfully, finding that this practice brought uninterrupted focus and a sense of calm to their daily life.

Introduction

IN A WORLD FILLED WITH constant notifications and interruptions, the Do Not Disturb (DND) mode on your devices can be a powerful tool to help you maintain focus and productivity. This chapter explores how to effectively use DND mode to minimize interruptions, enhance concentration, and improve work-life balance.

Understanding Do Not Disturb Mode

DO NOT DISTURB MODE is a feature available on most smartphones, tablets, and computers that silences notifications, calls, and alerts. Dr. Adam Gazzaley, a neuroscientist and author of *The Distracted Mind*, explains that minimizing interruptions is crucial for maintaining deep focus and cognitive performance.

Expert Insights and Research

RESEARCH FROM THE *Journal of Experimental Psychology* indicates that even brief interruptions can significantly impact cognitive performance and productivity. The study found that it can take up to 23 minutes to regain focus after being interrupted. Using DND mode can help create uninterrupted blocks of time for deep work.

Dr. Gloria Mark, a professor at the University of California, Irvine, emphasizes that reducing digital distractions is essential for maintaining mental well-being. Her research shows that frequent interruptions can lead to increased stress and decreased productivity.

Practical Steps and Tips

1. ENABLE DO NOT DISTURB Mode During Focused Work Sessions Activate DND mode during tasks that require deep focus and concentration. This helps create an interruption-free environment, allowing you to work more efficiently and effectively. Schedule regular blocks of time for focused work and use DND mode to minimize distractions.

2. Customize Your Do Not Disturb Settings Most devices allow you to customize DND settings to suit your needs. You can choose to allow calls and messages from specific contacts, set exceptions for urgent notifications, and schedule DND mode to activate automatically during certain times. Tailor the settings to create a balance between minimizing interruptions and staying accessible for important matters.

3. Use DND Mode for Personal Time Enable DND mode during personal time to reduce digital distractions and enhance your work-life balance. This includes mealtimes, family activities, exercise, and relaxation. Disconnecting from digital devices during these times can help you be more present and improve your overall well-being.

4. Schedule Regular Digital Detox Periods In addition to using DND mode, schedule regular digital detox periods where you completely disconnect from digital devices. Use this time to engage in offline activities, connect with loved ones, and recharge. Dr. Adam Gazzaley recommends incorporating digital detoxes into your routine to reduce digital overload and improve mental health.

Additional Tips for Mastering Do Not Disturb Mode

1. COMMUNICATE YOUR Availability Inform your colleagues, friends, and family about your DND schedule. Let them know when you'll be available and when you need uninterrupted time. Clear communication helps manage expectations and reduces the likelihood of disruptions.

2. Set Boundaries for Work and Personal Time Establish clear boundaries between work and personal time by using DND mode. For example, enable DND mode after work hours to disconnect from work-related notifications and focus on personal activities. Setting boundaries helps create a healthy work-life balance.

3. Use DND Mode for Meetings and Important Events Activate DND mode during meetings, presentations, and important events to ensure you remain focused and engaged. This prevents distractions and demonstrates respect for others' time.

4. Combine DND Mode with Other Focus Strategies Enhance the effectiveness of DND mode by combining it with other focus strategies, such as time-blocking, the Pomodoro Technique, and task prioritization. These techniques can help you stay organized and maximize productivity.

5. Regularly Review and Adjust Your DND Settings Regularly review and adjust your DND settings to ensure they continue to meet your needs. As your schedule and priorities change, update your settings to maintain a balance between minimizing interruptions and staying accessible for important matters.

Do's and Don'ts of Using Do Not Disturb Mode

DO'S:

• **Do enable DND mode during focused work sessions**: Create interruption-free blocks of time for deep work.

• **Do customize your DND settings**: Tailor settings to allow calls and messages from specific contacts and set exceptions for urgent notifications.

• **Do use DND mode for personal time**: Reduce digital distractions during meals, family activities, exercise, and relaxation.

• **Do schedule regular digital detox periods**: Disconnect from digital devices to recharge and improve mental health.

• **Do communicate your availability**: Inform colleagues, friends, and family about your DND schedule.

• **Do set boundaries for work and personal time**: Use DND mode to establish clear boundaries and create a healthy work-life balance.

• **Do use DND mode for meetings and important events**: Ensure focus and engagement by minimizing distractions.

• **Do combine DND mode with other focus strategies**: Enhance productivity by using time-blocking, the Pomodoro Technique, and task prioritization.

• **Do regularly review and adjust your DND settings**: Update settings as your schedule and priorities change.

Don'ts:

• **Don't ignore the need for focused work sessions**: Regularly schedule uninterrupted time for deep work.

• **Don't neglect to customize your settings**: Tailor DND settings to suit your needs and stay accessible for important matters.

• **Don't overlook the importance of personal time**: Use DND mode to disconnect from digital devices and be present in personal activities.

• **Don't forget to schedule digital detox periods**: Regularly disconnect from digital devices to reduce digital overload.

• **Don't avoid communicating your availability**: Inform others about your DND schedule to manage expectations.

• **Don't blur the lines between work and personal time**: Establish clear boundaries to maintain a healthy work-life balance.

• **Don't rely solely on DND mode**: Combine it with other focus strategies for maximum productivity.

• **Don't ignore the need to adjust your settings**: Regularly review and update your DND settings to match your changing needs.

FAQ: Mastering Do Not Disturb Mode

Q: WHAT IS DO NOT DISTURB mode? A: Do Not Disturb mode is a feature available on most smartphones, tablets, and computers that silences notifications, calls, and alerts to minimize interruptions and enhance focus.

Q: How can I customize my Do Not Disturb settings? A: Most devices allow you to customize DND settings to suit your needs. You can allow calls and messages from specific contacts, set exceptions for urgent notifications, and schedule DND mode to activate automatically during certain times.

Q: When should I use Do Not Disturb mode? A: Use DND mode during focused work sessions, personal time, meetings, presentations, and important events to minimize interruptions and maintain focus.

Q: How can Do Not Disturb mode improve my work-life balance? A: Enabling DND mode during personal time helps reduce digital distractions and allows you to be more present in personal activities, creating a healthier work-life balance.

Q: What are digital detox periods? A: Digital detox periods are scheduled times where you completely disconnect from digital devices to engage in offline activities, connect with loved ones, and recharge.

Q: How can I communicate my Do Not Disturb schedule to others? A: Inform your colleagues, friends, and family about your DND schedule and let them know when you'll be available and when you need uninterrupted time. Clear communication helps manage expectations and reduces disruptions.

Q: What are some other focus strategies to use with Do Not Disturb mode? A: Combine DND mode with time-blocking, the Pomodoro Technique, and task prioritization to enhance productivity and stay organized.

Case Studies and Examples

SOPHIA'S FOCUSED WORK Sessions Sophia, a marketing manager, struggled with constant interruptions from emails and notifications. She started using DND mode during her focused work sessions to create uninterrupted blocks of time. Sophia also customized her DND settings to allow calls from her supervisor and set exceptions for urgent notifications. These changes helped her maintain deep focus and significantly improved her productivity.

John's Personal Time Boundaries John, a software developer, found it challenging to disconnect from work-related notifications during personal time. He enabled DND mode after work hours and communicated his schedule to his team. John also set digital boundaries for screen use during meals and family activities. These practices helped him create a healthy work-life balance and be more present with his loved ones.

Rachel's Meeting Focus Rachel, a teacher, noticed that notifications during meetings and presentations distracted her and her students. She started using DND mode during all meetings and important events to minimize distractions. Rachel also encouraged her students to do the same during class. This approach improved focus and engagement for both her and her students.

Mark's Digital Detox Mark, a financial analyst, experienced digital overload from constant connectivity. He scheduled regular digital detox periods where he completely disconnected from his devices. During these times, Mark engaged in activities like hiking, reading, and spending time with friends. The digital detoxes helped him recharge, reduce stress, and improve his mental clarity.

Emily's Customized DND Settings Emily, a customer service representative, needed to balance being accessible for urgent matters while minimizing distractions. She customized her DND settings to allow calls and messages from specific contacts and set exceptions for urgent notifications. Emily also combined DND mode with time-blocking to organize her tasks. These adjustments helped her maintain focus and stay responsive to important matters.

Conclusion

MASTERING DO NOT DISTURB mode is essential for minimizing interruptions, enhancing concentration, and improving work-life balance. By enabling DND mode during focused work sessions, customizing your settings, using it for personal time, scheduling digital detox periods, and combining it with other focus strategies, you can take control of your digital life and achieve greater productivity and well-being. Implement these strategies to harness the power of DND mode and create an interruption-free environment.

Chapter 20: Remote Work Wellness Habits

T*he Bamboo Grove*

A remote worker, feeling isolated and weary, asked the master, "How can I maintain my well-being while working from home?"

The master led the worker to a bamboo grove and said, "Observe the bamboo."

The worker noticed that the bamboo stood tall, swaying gently in the breeze. Each stalk was rooted firmly in the ground, yet they all moved together in harmony with the wind.

The master explained, "Your work life should be like the bamboo—flexible yet grounded. Establish roots in routines that support your well-being, and sway with the changes and demands of your work."

The worker asked, "What habits should I cultivate?"

The master replied, "Begin with a dedicated workspace, regular breaks, and physical activity. Connect with others, maintain a balanced schedule, and nurture both mind and body. Let these habits be your roots."

The worker understood and began incorporating wellness habits into their remote work routine, finding balance and resilience like the bamboo in the grove

Introduction

REMOTE WORK HAS BECOME increasingly common, offering flexibility and convenience. However, it also presents unique challenges to maintaining wellness. This chapter explores essential habits for remote work wellness, focusing on creating a healthy and productive remote work environment.

Understanding Remote Work Wellness

REMOTE WORK WELLNESS involves adopting habits and practices that promote physical, mental, and emotional well-being while working from home. Dr. Karen Sobel Lojeski, an expert in virtual distance and remote work, emphasizes the importance of establishing routines and boundaries to maintain work-life balance and prevent burnout.

Expert Insights and Research

RESEARCH FROM THE *Journal of Occupational Health Psychology* highlights the importance of remote work wellness practices in reducing stress and improving productivity. The study found that individuals who implemented wellness habits experienced lower levels of fatigue and higher job satisfaction.

Dr. Nicholas Bloom, a professor of economics at Stanford University, has conducted extensive research on remote work. His findings suggest that remote workers who establish clear routines and maintain regular communication with colleagues are more productive and have better mental health outcomes.

Practical Steps and Tips

1. CREATE A DEDICATED Workspace Designate a specific area in your home for work to create a clear separation between work and personal life. Ensure your workspace is comfortable, well-lit, and equipped with necessary tools and technology. Dr. Karen Sobel Lojeski recommends setting up an ergonomic workstation to reduce physical strain and improve productivity.

2. Establish a Routine Develop a consistent daily routine to provide structure and maintain a sense of normalcy. Start your day at the same time, take regular breaks, and set specific work hours. Following a routine helps signal to your brain when it's time to work and when it's time to relax.

3. Take Regular Breaks Incorporate regular breaks into your workday to prevent burnout and maintain productivity. The Pomodoro Technique, which involves working for 25 minutes followed by a five-minute break, can help you stay focused and refreshed. Dr. Nicholas Bloom suggests taking short breaks every hour to stretch, hydrate, and rest your eyes.

4. Stay Physically Active Physical activity is essential for overall wellness. Schedule time for exercise, whether it's a morning run, midday yoga session, or evening walk. Physical activity helps reduce stress, boost energy levels, and improve mental health. The World Health Organization recommends at least 150 minutes of moderate-intensity exercise per week.

5. Maintain Social Connections Remote work can lead to feelings of isolation, so it's important to stay connected with colleagues, friends, and family. Schedule regular virtual meetings, video calls, and social activities to maintain social connections and support. Dr. Karen Sobel Lojeski's research emphasizes the importance of maintaining regular communication to reduce virtual distance and enhance collaboration.

Additional Tips for Remote Work Wellness

1. SET BOUNDARIES Establish clear boundaries between work and personal life to prevent work from encroaching on your personal time. Set specific work hours and communicate them to your colleagues and family. Create a ritual to signal the end of your workday, such as shutting down your computer or going for a walk.

2. Practice Mindfulness Incorporate mindfulness practices into your daily routine to reduce stress and improve focus. Techniques such as meditation, deep breathing, and journaling can help you stay present and manage stress. Use apps like Headspace or Calm for guided mindfulness sessions.

3. Prioritize Self-Care Make self-care a priority by scheduling time for activities that nourish your mind and body. This includes getting enough sleep, eating nutritious meals, staying hydrated, and engaging in hobbies. Dr. Nicholas Bloom's research suggests that prioritizing self-care can enhance productivity and overall well-being.

4. Optimize Your Technology Use Use technology to support your remote work wellness. This includes using productivity tools, setting up a reliable internet connection, and ensuring your devices are functioning properly. Explore apps and software that can enhance your workflow and reduce digital distractions.

5. Seek Support When Needed If you're struggling with the challenges of remote work, seek support from colleagues, supervisors, or mental health professionals. Many organizations offer resources and programs to support remote workers. Don't hesitate to reach out for help when needed.

Do's and Don'ts of Remote Work Wellness

DO'S:

- **Do create a dedicated workspace**: Designate a specific area in your home for work to create separation between work and personal life.

- **Do establish a routine**: Develop a consistent daily routine to provide structure and maintain normalcy.

- **Do take regular breaks**: Incorporate regular breaks into your workday to prevent burnout and maintain productivity.

- **Do stay physically active**: Schedule time for exercise to reduce stress and improve mental health.

- **Do maintain social connections**: Stay connected with colleagues, friends, and family through regular virtual meetings and social activities.

- **Do set boundaries**: Establish clear boundaries between work and personal life to prevent work from encroaching on your personal time.

- **Do practice mindfulness**: Incorporate mindfulness practices into your daily routine to reduce stress and improve focus.

- **Do prioritize self-care**: Schedule time for activities that nourish your mind and body, such as sleep, nutrition, hydration, and hobbies.

- **Do optimize your technology use**: Use technology to support your remote work wellness and enhance your workflow.

- **Do seek support when needed**: Reach out for help from colleagues, supervisors, or mental health professionals if you're struggling with remote work challenges.

Don'ts:

- **Don't work from bed or couch**: Create a dedicated workspace to maintain a clear separation between work and personal life.

- **Don't neglect your routine**: Stick to a consistent daily routine to provide structure and maintain normalcy.

- **Don't skip breaks**: Regular breaks are essential for preventing burnout and maintaining productivity.

- **Don't neglect physical activity**: Schedule regular exercise to reduce stress and improve mental health.

- **Don't isolate yourself**: Stay connected with colleagues, friends, and family through regular virtual meetings and social activities.

- **Don't blur the lines between work and personal life**: Establish clear boundaries to maintain a healthy work-life balance.

- **Don't ignore mindfulness practices**: Incorporate mindfulness techniques to reduce stress and improve focus.

- **Don't neglect self-care**: Prioritize activities that nourish your mind and body, such as sleep, nutrition, hydration, and hobbies.

- **Don't overlook technology optimization**: Use technology to support your remote work wellness and enhance your workflow.

- **Don't hesitate to seek support**: Reach out for help if you're struggling with remote work challenges.

FAQ: Remote Work Wellness

Q: WHAT IS REMOTE WORK wellness? A: Remote work wellness involves adopting habits and practices that promote physical, mental, and emotional well-being while working from home.

Q: How can I create a dedicated workspace? A: Designate a specific area in your home for work, ensure it's comfortable and well-lit, and set up an ergonomic workstation to reduce physical strain and improve productivity.

Q: Why is it important to establish a routine for remote work? A: A consistent daily routine provides structure, signals to your brain when it's time to work and relax, and helps maintain a sense of normalcy.

Q: What are the benefits of taking regular breaks during remote work? A: Regular breaks prevent burnout, maintain productivity, reduce physical strain, and improve mental well-being.

Q: How can I stay physically active while working remotely? A: Schedule regular exercise sessions, such as morning runs, midday yoga, or evening walks, to reduce stress and improve mental health.

Q: Why is it important to maintain social connections while working remotely? A: Staying connected with colleagues, friends, and family through regular virtual meetings and social activities helps prevent feelings of isolation and supports mental well-being.

Q: How can I set boundaries between work and personal life while working remotely? A: Establish clear work hours, communicate them to colleagues and family, and create a ritual to signal the end of your workday, such as shutting down your computer or going for a walk.

Q: What are some mindfulness practices for remote work wellness? A: Techniques such as meditation, deep breathing, and journaling can help reduce stress, improve focus, and promote mental well-being.

Q: How can I optimize my technology use for remote work wellness? A: Use productivity tools, ensure a reliable internet connection, and explore apps and software that enhance your workflow and reduce digital distractions.

Q: What should I do if I'm struggling with remote work challenges? A: Seek support from colleagues, supervisors, or mental health professionals. Many organizations offer resources and programs to support remote workers.

Case Studies and Examples

SOPHIA'S STRUCTURED Routine Sophia, a marketing manager, initially struggled with the lack of structure in remote work. She developed a consistent daily routine, starting her day at the same time and taking regular breaks using the Pomodoro Technique. Sophia also created a dedicated workspace and scheduled time for exercise and social activities. These changes helped her maintain a sense of normalcy and improved her productivity and well-being.

John's Social Connections John, a software developer, felt isolated working remotely and missed interacting with colleagues. He scheduled regular virtual meetings and social activities with his team, such as virtual coffee breaks and online game nights. John also stayed connected with friends and family through video calls and social media. These efforts helped him feel more connected and supported.

Rachel's Mindfulness Practice Rachel, a teacher, experienced stress and burnout from the demands of remote teaching. She incorporated mindfulness practices into her daily routine, such as morning meditation and evening journaling. Rachel also used the Headspace app for guided mindfulness sessions. These practices helped her manage stress, improve focus, and enhance her overall well-being.

Mark's Ergonomic Workspace Mark, a financial analyst, developed physical strain from working long hours at home. He set up an ergonomic workstation with a comfortable chair, adjustable desk, and proper lighting. Mark also took regular breaks to stretch and used a standing desk for part of the day. These adjustments reduced his physical discomfort and improved his productivity.

Emily's Self-Care Routine Emily, a customer service representative, found it challenging to balance work and personal life. She prioritized self-care by scheduling time for activities that nourished her mind and body, such as getting enough sleep, eating nutritious meals, staying hydrated, and engaging in hobbies like painting and gardening. These efforts helped Emily maintain a healthy work-life balance and improved her overall well-being.

Conclusion

ADOPTING WELLNESS HABITS is essential for maintaining physical, mental, and emotional well-being while working remotely. By creating a dedicated workspace, establishing a routine, taking regular breaks, staying physically active, maintaining social connections, setting boundaries, practicing mindfulness, prioritizing self-care, optimizing technology use, and seeking support when needed, you can create a healthy and productive remote work environment. Implement these strategies to enhance your remote work experience and achieve greater well-being.

Chapter 21: Digital Day Mindfulness Practices

The Steady Flame

A busy professional, distracted by the constant demands of digital life, asked the master, "How can I maintain mindfulness throughout my hectic digital day?"

The master took the professional to a quiet room and lit a single candle. "Observe the flame," the master said.

The flame flickered slightly but remained steady, illuminating the room with a soft, unwavering light. The master explained, "This flame represents your awareness. Despite the surrounding distractions, it stays steady and bright."

The professional asked, "How can I keep my awareness like this flame?"

The master replied, "Begin each day by lighting your inner flame with a moment of mindfulness. Throughout the day, return to this flame with brief pauses. Focus on your breath, center your thoughts, and let the flame guide you."

The professional understood and started incorporating mindful pauses into their digital day, finding that these moments of focus kept their inner flame steady and their mind clear amidst the chaos.

Introduction

INCORPORATING MINDFULNESS into your daily digital routine can help reduce stress, increase focus, and improve overall well-being. This chapter explores mindfulness practices specifically tailored for the digital age, offering strategies to maintain a healthy relationship with technology.

Understanding Digital Mindfulness

DIGITAL MINDFULNESS involves being present and intentional with your technology use, reducing distractions, and fostering a sense of balance. Dr. Jon Kabat-Zinn, the pioneer of mindfulness-based stress reduction (MBSR), explains that mindfulness can be practiced in any context, including our interactions with digital devices.

Expert Insights and Research

RESEARCH FROM THE *Journal of Cognitive Enhancement* indicates that mindfulness practices can enhance cognitive function, reduce stress, and improve emotional regulation. The study found that individuals who incorporated mindfulness into their daily routines experienced greater focus and mental clarity.

Dr. Mark Williams, a professor at the University of Oxford and co-author of *Mindfulness: A Practical Guide to Finding Peace in a Frantic World*, emphasizes that mindfulness can help us navigate the challenges of the digital age, promoting a healthier relationship with technology.

Practical Steps and Tips

1. START YOUR DAY WITH Mindfulness Begin your day with a mindfulness practice to set a positive tone. This could be a few minutes of meditation, deep breathing, or mindful stretching. Apps like Headspace or Calm offer guided sessions to help you get started. Dr. Jon Kabat-Zinn recommends starting with just five minutes each morning.

2. Practice Mindful Breathing During Breaks Take mindful breathing breaks throughout your day to reduce stress and refocus. Set a timer to remind yourself to take a few deep breaths every hour. Dr. Mark Williams suggests using a simple technique like box breathing (inhale for four counts, hold for four, exhale for four, hold for four) to calm the mind.

3. Implement Mindful Screen Use Be intentional with your screen time by setting specific goals for each digital interaction. Avoid mindlessly scrolling through social media or checking emails out of habit. Dr. Jon Kabat-Zinn advises pausing before you engage with your device to set a clear intention for its use.

4. Create Tech-Free Moments Designate specific times of the day to disconnect from digital devices. This could include meal times, during exercise, or before bed. Creating tech-free moments helps you stay present and engage more fully in offline activities.

5. Practice Digital Mindfulness Meditations Incorporate digital mindfulness meditations into your routine to cultivate a balanced relationship with technology. Apps like Insight Timer and 10% Happier offer meditations specifically designed for digital mindfulness. These sessions can help you become more aware of your digital habits and make intentional choices.

Additional Tips for Digital Day Mindfulness

1. USE MINDFULNESS Prompts Set reminders or use mindfulness prompts on your devices to bring your attention back to the present moment. This could be a gentle chime, a notification to take a deep breath, or a prompt to check in with your body.

2. Engage in Mindful Listening When listening to music, podcasts, or videos, practice mindful listening by focusing fully on the sounds. Avoid multitasking and allow yourself to fully experience the audio content.

3. Practice Gratitude Take a few moments each day to express gratitude for the positive aspects of your digital life. This could include appreciating the convenience of technology, the ability to connect with loved ones, or access to information and resources.

4. Conduct a Digital Detox Schedule regular digital detox periods where you completely disconnect from digital devices. Use this time to engage in offline activities, connect with nature, and recharge. Dr. Mark Williams recommends digital detoxes to reset your relationship with technology.

5. Reflect on Your Digital Habits Regularly reflect on your digital habits to identify areas for improvement. Keep a journal to document your observations and set goals for mindful technology use.

Do's and Don'ts of Digital Day Mindfulness

DO'S:

- **Do start your day with mindfulness**: Begin each day with a mindfulness practice to set a positive tone.

- **Do practice mindful breathing during breaks**: Take regular breathing breaks to reduce stress and refocus.

- **Do implement mindful screen use**: Be intentional with your screen time and set specific goals for digital interactions.

- **Do create tech-free moments**: Designate specific times to disconnect from digital devices and stay present.

- **Do practice digital mindfulness meditations**: Use guided meditations to cultivate a balanced relationship with technology.

- **Do use mindfulness prompts**: Set reminders to bring your attention back to the present moment.

- **Do engage in mindful listening**: Focus fully on audio content and avoid multitasking.

- **Do practice gratitude**: Express gratitude for the positive aspects of your digital life.

- **Do conduct regular digital detoxes**: Schedule periods to completely disconnect from digital devices and recharge.

- **Do reflect on your digital habits**: Regularly review your digital habits and set goals for improvement.

Don'ts:

- **Don't start your day with screens**: Begin your day with mindfulness instead of immediately checking your phone or computer.

- **Don't skip breathing breaks**: Regular breaks are essential for reducing stress and maintaining focus.

- **Don't engage in mindless screen use**: Avoid using digital devices out of habit and be intentional with your interactions.

- **Don't neglect tech-free moments**: Ensure you have designated times to disconnect from digital devices.

- **Don't overlook digital mindfulness meditations**: Incorporate these meditations to enhance your relationship with technology.

- **Don't ignore mindfulness prompts**: Use reminders to stay present and mindful throughout the day.

- **Don't multitask while listening**: Practice mindful listening by fully focusing on audio content.

- **Don't forget to express gratitude**: Take time to appreciate the positive aspects of your digital life.

- **Don't avoid digital detoxes**: Regularly disconnect from digital devices to reset your relationship with technology.

- **Don't neglect reflection**: Regularly review and adjust your digital habits for continuous improvement.

FAQ: Digital Day Mindfulness Practices

Q: WHAT IS DIGITAL mindfulness? A: Digital mindfulness involves being present and intentional with your technology use, reducing distractions, and fostering a sense of balance in your digital interactions.

Q: How can I start my day with mindfulness? A: Begin your day with a mindfulness practice such as meditation, deep breathing, or mindful stretching. Use apps like Headspace or Calm for guided sessions.

Q: What are some effective breathing exercises for mindfulness? A: Effective breathing exercises include deep diaphragmatic breathing and box breathing. These techniques can help reduce stress and refocus the mind.

Q: How can I practice mindful screen use? A: Be intentional with your screen time by setting specific goals for each digital interaction and avoiding mindless scrolling or checking emails out of habit.

Q: What are tech-free moments? A: Tech-free moments are designated times of the day when you disconnect from digital devices to stay present and engage fully in offline activities.

Q: How can I incorporate digital mindfulness meditations into my routine? A: Use apps like Insight Timer and 10% Happier for guided meditations specifically designed for digital mindfulness. These sessions can help you become more aware of your digital habits.

Q: What are mindfulness prompts? A: Mindfulness prompts are reminders or notifications on your devices that bring your attention back to the present moment, encouraging mindful technology use.

Q: Why is it important to practice gratitude for digital life? A: Practicing gratitude helps you appreciate the positive aspects of your digital interactions and fosters a balanced relationship with technology.

Q: What is a digital detox? A: A digital detox is a scheduled period where you completely disconnect from digital devices to engage in offline activities, connect with nature, and recharge.

Q: How can I reflect on my digital habits? A: Keep a journal to document your digital habits, identify areas for improvement, and set goals for mindful technology use.

Case Studies and Examples

SOPHIA'S MORNING MINDFULNESS Sophia, a project manager, found that starting her day with a mindfulness practice significantly improved her focus and reduced stress. She used the Calm app for a 10-minute guided meditation each morning. This routine helped her set a positive tone for the day and approach her digital interactions with intention.

John's Mindful Breathing Breaks John, a marketing executive, incorporated mindful breathing breaks into his workday. He set a timer to remind him to take a few deep breaths every hour, using the box breathing technique. These breaks helped John stay calm, focused, and productive throughout the day.

Rachel's Tech-Free Meals Rachel, a teacher, designated mealtimes as tech-free moments to disconnect from digital devices and be present with her family. She noticed that these tech-free meals improved her relationships and allowed her to enjoy her food more mindfully.

Mark's Digital Detox Weekends Mark, a financial analyst, scheduled regular digital detox weekends where he completely disconnected from his devices. During these weekends, Mark engaged in activities like hiking, reading, and spending time with friends. The digital detoxes helped him recharge and improve his mental clarity.

Emily's Digital Reflection Journal Emily, a customer service representative, kept a digital reflection journal to document her technology use and set goals for mindful interactions. She used the Day One app to record her observations and reflections. This practice helped Emily become more aware of her digital habits and make intentional choices.

Conclusion

INCORPORATING MINDFULNESS into your daily digital routine can help you maintain a healthy relationship with technology, reduce stress, and improve overall well-being. By starting your day with mindfulness, practicing mindful breathing, being intentional with screen use, creating tech-free moments, and reflecting on your digital habits, you can cultivate a balanced digital lifestyle. Implement these strategies to enhance your focus, mental clarity, and overall happiness in the digital age.

Chapter 22: Technology for Enhancing Sleep

T*he Gentle Waves*

A restless seeker, struggling with sleepless nights, asked the sage, "How can technology help me find restful sleep?"

The sage led the seeker to the edge of a tranquil lake. "Listen to the waves," the sage said.

The seeker listened as the gentle waves lapped rhythmically against the shore, creating a soothing sound. The sage explained, "These waves are like the calming technology you can use to enhance your sleep."

The seeker asked, "What technology should I use?"

The sage replied, "Embrace tools that mimic the rhythm of these waves. Use white noise machines, calming music apps, and blue light filters. Let these technologies create a peaceful environment, just as the waves bring calm to the lake."

The seeker understood and began using technology mindfully to enhance their sleep, finding that the gentle rhythms of sound and light helped them drift into restful slumber, like the soothing waves of the lake

Introduction

IN THE DIGITAL AGE, technology can be both a boon and a bane for our sleep. While screens and constant connectivity can disrupt sleep patterns, certain technologies can also help enhance sleep quality. This chapter explores various tech solutions that can improve your sleep hygiene and overall rest.

Understanding Sleep and Technology

GOOD SLEEP HYGIENE involves practices that support consistent, quality sleep. Dr. Matthew Walker, a renowned sleep scientist and author of *Why We Sleep*, emphasizes the importance of maintaining a regular sleep schedule and creating an environment conducive to rest. Technology, when used mindfully, can play a significant role in enhancing sleep.

Expert Insights and Research

RESEARCH FROM THE *Journal of Clinical Sleep Medicine* indicates that while excessive screen time before bed can negatively impact sleep, certain technologies, such as blue light filters and sleep tracking devices, can improve sleep quality. Dr. Walker's research also highlights the benefits of using technology to monitor sleep patterns and implement effective sleep hygiene practices.

Practical Steps and Tips

1. USE BLUE LIGHT FILTERS Blue light emitted by screens can interfere with the production of melatonin, a hormone that regulates sleep. Use blue light filters on your devices to reduce exposure in the evening. Many smartphones, tablets, and computers have built-in blue light filtering features, such as Night Shift on Apple devices or Night Mode on Android devices.

2. Invest in a Sleep Tracking Device Sleep tracking devices, such as the Fitbit, Oura Ring, and Apple Watch, can monitor your sleep patterns and provide insights into your sleep quality. These devices track metrics like sleep duration, sleep stages, and heart rate variability. Dr. Matthew Walker suggests using sleep tracking data to identify areas for improvement and make necessary adjustments to your sleep routine.

3. Create a Relaxing Bedtime Routine Incorporate technology into your bedtime routine to promote relaxation. Apps like Calm and Headspace offer guided meditations, sleep stories, and breathing exercises designed to help you unwind. Dr. Walker recommends establishing a consistent pre-sleep routine to signal to your body that it's time to wind down.

4. Optimize Your Sleep Environment Use technology to create a sleep-friendly environment. Smart home devices like smart lights and thermostats can help you adjust lighting and temperature to optimal levels for sleep. White noise machines or apps can also provide soothing sounds to mask disruptive noises and promote restful sleep.

Additional Tips for Enhancing Sleep with Technology

1. LIMIT SCREEN TIME Before Bed While technology can aid sleep, it's important to limit screen time before bed to reduce exposure to blue light and mental stimulation. Aim to turn off screens at least one hour before bedtime. Use this time to engage in relaxing activities like reading or gentle stretching.

2. Utilize Sleep Apps There are numerous apps designed to enhance sleep quality. Apps like Sleep Cycle and Pillow use your device's sensors to monitor sleep patterns and provide detailed reports on your sleep quality. These apps can also offer smart alarms that wake you up during the lightest sleep phase, making it easier to start your day.

3. Manage Stress and Anxiety Stress and anxiety are common barriers to good sleep. Use apps like Breethe or Insight Timer for guided meditations, breathing exercises, and mindfulness practices that can help reduce stress and promote relaxation before bed.

4. Sync with Health Platforms Many sleep tracking devices can sync with health platforms like Apple Health, Google Fit, and Fitbit. This integration allows you to track sleep alongside other health metrics, providing a comprehensive view of your well-being. Use this data to make informed decisions about your health and sleep habits.

5. Set Sleep Goals Use your sleep tracking device to set specific sleep goals and monitor your progress. Whether it's increasing your total sleep time, improving sleep efficiency, or reducing nighttime awakenings, setting goals can help you stay motivated and focused on improving your sleep hygiene.

Do's and Don'ts of Using Technology for Sleep

DO'S:

- **Do use blue light filters**: Reduce blue light exposure in the evening to support melatonin production and better sleep.

- **Do invest in a sleep tracking device**: Monitor your sleep patterns and use the data to improve your sleep hygiene.

- **Do create a relaxing bedtime routine**: Incorporate guided meditations, sleep stories, and breathing exercises into your pre-sleep routine.

- **Do optimize your sleep environment**: Use smart home devices to adjust lighting and temperature, and consider white noise machines or apps for a soothing sleep environment.

- **Do limit screen time before bed**: Turn off screens at least one hour before bedtime to reduce blue light exposure and mental stimulation.

- **Do utilize sleep apps**: Use apps designed to enhance sleep quality and provide detailed reports on your sleep patterns.

- **Do manage stress and anxiety**: Use mindfulness and meditation apps to reduce stress and promote relaxation before bed.

- **Do sync with health platforms**: Integrate sleep tracking devices with health platforms to monitor overall well-being.

- **Do set sleep goals**: Use your sleep tracking device to set and monitor specific sleep goals.

Don'ts:

- **Don't ignore blue light exposure**: Failing to use blue light filters can disrupt melatonin production and impair sleep.

- **Don't overlook the importance of a bedtime routine**: Establishing a consistent pre-sleep routine is crucial for signaling to your body that it's time to wind down.

- **Don't neglect your sleep environment**: Optimizing your sleep environment is essential for promoting restful sleep.

- **Don't use screens right before bed**: Limit screen time before bed to reduce blue light exposure and mental stimulation.

- **Don't forget to track your progress**: Regularly monitor your sleep patterns and adjust your habits to improve sleep quality.

- **Don't ignore stress and anxiety**: Managing stress and anxiety is crucial for promoting relaxation and better sleep.

- **Don't rely solely on technology**: While technology can aid sleep, it's important to also practice good sleep hygiene habits.

FAQ: Technology for Enhancing Sleep

Q: HOW DOES BLUE LIGHT affect sleep? A: Blue light emitted by screens can interfere with the production of melatonin, a hormone that regulates sleep. Reducing blue light exposure in the evening can support better sleep.

Q: What are sleep tracking devices? A: Sleep tracking devices, such as the Fitbit, Oura Ring, and Apple Watch, monitor sleep patterns and provide insights into sleep quality. These devices track metrics like sleep duration, sleep stages, and heart rate variability.

Q: How can I create a relaxing bedtime routine? A: Incorporate technology like guided meditation apps, sleep stories, and breathing exercises into your bedtime routine to promote relaxation. Establish a consistent pre-sleep routine to signal to your body that it's time to wind down.

Q: What are some ways to optimize my sleep environment? A: Use smart home devices like smart lights and thermostats to adjust lighting and temperature to optimal levels for sleep. Consider using white noise machines or apps to provide soothing sounds and mask disruptive noises.

Q: Why is it important to limit screen time before bed? A: Limiting screen time before bed reduces exposure to blue light and mental stimulation, which can improve sleep quality. Aim to turn off screens at least one hour before bedtime.

Q: How can mindfulness apps help with sleep? A: Mindfulness apps like Breethe and Insight Timer offer guided meditations, breathing exercises, and mindfulness practices that can reduce stress and promote relaxation before bed.

Q: How do sleep apps work? A: Sleep apps like Sleep Cycle and Pillow use your device's sensors to monitor sleep patterns and provide detailed reports on sleep quality. They can also offer smart alarms that wake you up during the lightest sleep phase.

Q: What are sleep goals, and why are they important? A: Sleep goals are specific objectives related to sleep, such as increasing total sleep time or improving sleep efficiency. Setting and monitoring sleep goals can help you stay motivated and focused on improving sleep hygiene.

Case Studies and Examples

SOPHIA'S BLUE LIGHT Filter Use Sophia, a project manager, noticed that she struggled to fall asleep after working late on her computer. She started using the Night Shift feature on her Apple devices to reduce blue light exposure in the evenings. Sophia also turned off screens an hour before bed and used a guided meditation app to relax. These changes improved her sleep quality and helped her fall asleep more easily.

John's Sleep Tracking Insights John, a marketing executive, invested in an Oura Ring to monitor his sleep patterns. He discovered that he was waking up frequently during the night. Using the data from his sleep tracker, John adjusted his bedtime routine and optimized his sleep environment by lowering the temperature and using a white noise machine. These adjustments led to more restful sleep and better overall health.

Rachel's Relaxing Bedtime Routine Rachel, a teacher, struggled with stress and difficulty falling asleep. She incorporated the Calm app into her bedtime routine, listening to sleep stories and guided meditations each night. Rachel also used a smart thermostat to adjust her bedroom temperature to a comfortable level. These practices helped her relax and improve her sleep quality.

Mark's Screen Time Management Mark, a financial analyst, found that excessive screen time before bed was impacting his sleep. He set a rule to turn off all screens an hour before bedtime and used that time to read a book or practice gentle stretching. Mark also used a sleep app to monitor his sleep patterns and set goals for improving his sleep hygiene. These changes helped him sleep more soundly and wake up feeling refreshed.

Emily's Stress Management Emily, a customer service representative, experienced stress and anxiety that affected her sleep. She started using the Insight Timer app for guided meditations and breathing exercises before bed. Emily also kept a sleep journal to track her sleep patterns and identify stressors. These practices helped her manage stress and significantly improved her sleep quality.

Conclusion

TECHNOLOGY, WHEN USED mindfully, can play a significant role in enhancing sleep quality. By using blue light filters, investing in sleep tracking devices, creating a relaxing bedtime routine, optimizing your sleep environment, and managing stress, you can improve your sleep hygiene and overall rest. Implement these strategies to harness the power of technology for better sleep and enjoy the benefits of restful, rejuvenating nights.

Chapter 23: Practicing Comprehensive Digital Mindfulness

T*he Flowing River*

A tech-savvy disciple, feeling overwhelmed by the constant flow of digital information, asked the master, "How can I practice mindfulness in every aspect of my digital life?"

The master took the disciple to a riverbank and said, "Observe the river."

The disciple saw the river flowing smoothly, effortlessly navigating around rocks and obstacles. The master explained, "The river flows continuously, yet it remains mindful of its path, adapting to the terrain without losing its essence."

The disciple asked, "How can I be like the river in my digital life?"

The master replied, "Embrace the flow of digital information, but do so mindfully. Set intentions for your digital activities, take regular breaks to reflect, and adapt to changes without getting swept away. Let your actions be deliberate, like the river's course."

The disciple understood and began practicing comprehensive digital mindfulness, finding balance and peace in the constant flow of their digital interactions, much like the steady, mindful flow of the river.

Introduction

IN AN ERA DOMINATED by digital devices and constant connectivity, practicing comprehensive digital mindfulness can help maintain mental clarity, reduce stress, and foster a healthier relationship with technology. This chapter explores the principles of digital mindfulness and offers practical strategies to integrate mindful practices into your digital life.

Understanding Comprehensive Digital Mindfulness

COMPREHENSIVE DIGITAL mindfulness involves being fully present and aware of your interactions with technology. It encourages intentional use of digital devices, minimizing distractions, and promoting a balanced digital lifestyle. Dr. Jon Kabat-Zinn, a pioneer in mindfulness, emphasizes that mindfulness can be practiced in any context, including our digital interactions.

Expert Insights and Research

RESEARCH FROM THE *Journal of Behavioral Addictions* highlights the benefits of digital mindfulness practices in reducing technology-related stress and improving well-being. The study found that individuals who practiced digital mindfulness experienced lower levels of anxiety and greater satisfaction with their technology use.

Dr. Mark Williams, a professor at the University of Oxford and co-author of *Mindfulness: A Practical Guide to Finding Peace in a Frantic World*, explains that digital mindfulness can help individuals navigate the complexities of the digital age, leading to improved focus, reduced stress, and enhanced overall well-being.

Practical Steps and Tips

1. START WITH A DIGITAL Mindfulness Meditation Begin your journey into digital mindfulness with a guided meditation specifically designed to enhance awareness of your technology use. Apps like Insight Timer and Headspace offer digital mindfulness meditations that can help you become more aware of your digital habits and make intentional choices.

2. Set Intentions for Digital Use Before engaging with your devices, set clear intentions for what you want to achieve. This helps prevent mindless scrolling and encourages purposeful interactions. Dr. Jon Kabat-Zinn suggests taking a moment to pause and reflect before using any digital device to ensure intentional use.

3. Practice the Digital Detox Regularly disconnect from digital devices to recharge and reconnect with the physical world. Schedule digital detox periods where you completely unplug, allowing yourself to engage in offline activities and rest your mind. Dr. Mark Williams recommends incorporating digital detoxes into your routine to reset your relationship with technology.

4. Use Mindfulness Prompts Set reminders or use mindfulness prompts to bring your attention back to the present moment. These can be gentle chimes, notifications, or visual cues that encourage you to take a deep breath and refocus. Apps like MindBell can provide regular mindfulness reminders throughout the day.

5. Cultivate a Mindful Digital Environment Create a digital environment that supports mindfulness by decluttering your devices and organizing your digital space. Remove unnecessary apps, organize files, and use calming backgrounds to reduce digital stress. A clean and organized digital environment can enhance focus and reduce distractions.

Additional Tips for Practicing Comprehensive Digital Mindfulness

1. MINDFUL EMAIL MANAGEMENT Practice mindfulness when managing your emails by setting specific times to check and respond to messages. Avoid constantly checking your inbox and focus on completing one task at a time. Use email management tools to organize and prioritize your messages.

2. Mindful Social Media Use Be intentional with your social media interactions by setting limits on usage and focusing on meaningful connections. Unfollow or mute accounts that do not add value to your life and engage with content that inspires and uplifts you. Use social media mindfully to enhance your well-being.

3. Practice Mindful Breathing Incorporate mindful breathing exercises into your daily routine to reduce stress and improve focus. Set a timer to remind yourself to take a few deep breaths every hour. Techniques like box breathing (inhale for four counts, hold for four, exhale for four, hold for four) can help calm the mind.

4. Engage in Mindful Listening When consuming digital content, such as music, podcasts, or videos, practice mindful listening by fully focusing on the audio experience. Avoid multitasking and allow yourself to be fully present with the content. This can enhance your enjoyment and understanding of the material.

5. Reflect on Your Digital Habits Regularly reflect on your digital habits to identify areas for improvement. Keep a digital mindfulness journal to document your observations, set goals, and track your progress. Reflecting on your digital interactions can help you make more intentional and mindful choices.

Do's and Don'ts of Comprehensive Digital Mindfulness
DO'S:

• **Do start with digital mindfulness meditations**: Use guided meditations to enhance awareness of your technology use.

• **Do set intentions for digital use**: Reflect on your goals before engaging with your devices to ensure intentional interactions.

• **Do practice regular digital detoxes**: Schedule periods to completely disconnect from digital devices and recharge.

• **Do use mindfulness prompts**: Set reminders to bring your attention back to the present moment and reduce distractions.

• **Do cultivate a mindful digital environment**: Declutter your devices and organize your digital space for enhanced focus.

• **Do practice mindful email management**: Set specific times to check and respond to emails, and avoid constant inbox checking.

• **Do be intentional with social media use**: Set limits on usage, unfollow non-value-adding accounts, and engage with meaningful content.

- **Do incorporate mindful breathing exercises**: Use techniques like box breathing to reduce stress and improve focus.

- **Do engage in mindful listening**: Fully focus on digital content without multitasking to enhance your experience.

- **Do reflect on your digital habits**: Keep a digital mindfulness journal to track your progress and set intentional goals.

Don'ts:

- **Don't use devices mindlessly**: Avoid engaging with digital devices out of habit and be intentional with your interactions.

- **Don't neglect digital detox periods**: Regularly disconnect from digital devices to reset your relationship with technology.

- **Don't ignore mindfulness prompts**: Use reminders to stay present and reduce digital distractions.

- **Don't allow digital clutter**: Keep your digital environment organized to enhance focus and reduce stress.

- **Don't constantly check emails**: Set specific times for email management to avoid constant interruptions.

- **Don't mindlessly scroll through social media**: Be intentional with your social media interactions and set usage limits.

- **Don't forget to breathe**: Regularly practice mindful breathing exercises to reduce stress and improve focus.

- **Don't multitask while listening to digital content**: Practice mindful listening by fully focusing on audio experiences.

- **Don't neglect reflection**: Regularly review your digital habits and set goals for improvement.

FAQ: Practicing Comprehensive Digital Mindfulness

Q: WHAT IS COMPREHENSIVE digital mindfulness? A: Comprehensive digital mindfulness involves being fully present and aware of your interactions with technology, minimizing distractions, and promoting a balanced digital lifestyle.

Q: How can I start practicing digital mindfulness? A: Begin with guided digital mindfulness meditations available on apps like Insight Timer and Headspace. Set clear intentions for your digital use and regularly disconnect from devices through digital detoxes.

Q: What are digital detox periods? A: Digital detox periods are scheduled times where you completely unplug from digital devices to engage in offline activities and rest your mind.

Q: How can mindfulness prompts help with digital mindfulness? A: Mindfulness prompts are reminders or visual cues that bring your attention back to the present moment, encouraging mindful interactions with technology.

Q: How can I create a mindful digital environment? A: Declutter your devices by removing unnecessary apps and organizing your digital space. Use calming backgrounds and keep your devices organized to reduce digital stress.

Q: What is mindful email management? A: Mindful email management involves setting specific times to check and respond to emails, avoiding constant inbox checking, and using email management tools to organize and prioritize messages.

Q: How can I practice mindful social media use? A: Be intentional with your social media interactions by setting usage limits, unfollowing accounts that do not add value, and engaging with meaningful content.

Q: What are mindful breathing exercises? A: Mindful breathing exercises, such as box breathing, involve taking slow, deep breaths to reduce stress and improve focus. Set reminders to practice these exercises regularly.

Q: How can I practice mindful listening? A: Engage in mindful listening by fully focusing on digital content, such as music or podcasts, without multitasking. This enhances your experience and understanding of the material.

Q: Why is reflection important in digital mindfulness? A: Regularly reflecting on your digital habits helps you identify areas for improvement, set goals, and make more intentional and mindful choices.

Case Studies and Examples

SOPHIA'S MINDFUL DIGITAL Detox Sophia, a project manager, struggled with digital overload and constant connectivity. She scheduled regular digital detox periods where she completely disconnected from her devices. During these times, Sophia engaged in activities like hiking, painting, and spending time with loved ones. The digital detoxes helped her recharge and foster a healthier relationship with technology.

John's Intentional Email Management John, a marketing executive, found himself constantly checking emails throughout the day, leading to stress and decreased productivity. He set specific times to check and respond to emails and used an email management tool to organize and prioritize messages. These changes helped John manage his email more effectively and reduce stress.

Rachel's Social Media Mindfulness Rachel, a teacher, noticed that mindlessly scrolling through social media was affecting her mental well-being. She set limits on her social media usage and unfollowed accounts that did not add value. Rachel also engaged with content that inspired and uplifted her. These practices improved her social media experience and enhanced her well-being.

Mark's Mindful Listening Practice Mark, a financial analyst, enjoyed listening to podcasts but often found himself multitasking during episodes. He started practicing mindful listening by fully focusing on the audio content without distractions. Mark found that this enhanced his enjoyment and understanding of the material.

Emily's Digital Mindfulness Journal Emily, a customer service representative, kept a digital mindfulness journal to track her technology use and set goals for improvement. She used the journal to document her observations, reflect on her digital habits, and make intentional choices. This practice helped Emily cultivate a more mindful and balanced digital lifestyle.

Conclusion

PRACTICING COMPREHENSIVE digital mindfulness can help you maintain mental clarity, reduce stress, and foster a healthier relationship with technology. By starting with digital mindfulness meditations, setting intentions for digital use, practicing regular digital detoxes, using mindfulness prompts, and reflecting on your digital habits, you can create a balanced and mindful digital lifestyle. Implement these strategies to enhance your well-being and navigate the complexities of the digital age with greater ease.

Chapter 24: Designing Tech-Free Sanctuaries

The Quiet Forest

A devoted practitioner, seeking refuge from constant connectivity, asked the master, "How can I create a space free from technology where I can truly rest?"

The master led the practitioner to a dense, quiet forest. "Listen to the forest," the master said.

In the stillness, the practitioner heard only the gentle rustle of leaves and the distant call of birds. The master explained, "This forest is a sanctuary, free from the distractions of the outside world. It offers peace and renewal."

The practitioner asked, "How can I create such a sanctuary in my home?"

The master replied, "Designate a space where no technology enters. Fill it with natural elements, comforting textures, and items that bring you peace. Visit this sanctuary regularly to disconnect and renew your spirit, just as you find peace in the quiet forest."

The practitioner understood and began designing a tech-free sanctuary, finding solace and rejuvenation in a space dedicated to tranquility, much like the serene forest

Introduction

IN OUR INCREASINGLY connected world, creating tech-free sanctuaries—spaces without digital devices—can significantly improve mental clarity, reduce stress, and enhance overall well-being. This chapter explores how to design and maintain these tech-free zones in your home or workspace.

Understanding Tech-Free Sanctuaries

A TECH-FREE SANCTUARY is a designated space where digital devices are not allowed. These spaces are intended to provide a respite from the constant connectivity and digital distractions that characterize modern life. Dr. Sherry Turkle, a professor at MIT and author of *Alone Together*, emphasizes the importance of creating tech-free zones to foster meaningful interactions and promote mental well-being.

Expert Insights and Research

RESEARCH FROM THE *Journal of Environmental Psychology* indicates that tech-free spaces can reduce cognitive overload and improve focus. The study found that individuals who spent time in tech-free zones experienced lower levels of stress and higher levels of productivity.

Dr. Nicholas Carr, author of *The Shallows: What the Internet Is Doing to Our Brains*, explains that constant digital stimulation can fragment attention and impede deep thinking. Creating tech-free sanctuaries can help mitigate these effects and support mental clarity.

Additional research by Dr. Gloria Mark, a professor of informatics at the University of California, Irvine, highlights that constant task switching, often prompted by digital notifications, can increase stress and reduce productivity. Dr. Mark's work emphasizes the value of uninterrupted time in tech-free zones to restore focus and reduce mental fatigue.

Practical Steps and Tips

1. IDENTIFY TECH-FREE Zones Determine which areas of your home or workspace will be designated as tech-free sanctuaries. Common choices include bedrooms, dining rooms, and living areas. Dr. Sherry Turkle suggests starting with small, manageable spaces and gradually expanding tech-free zones.

2. Set Clear Boundaries Establish clear rules for your tech-free zones. Communicate these boundaries to family members, roommates, or colleagues to ensure everyone understands and respects the purpose of these spaces. Consider creating visual reminders, such as signs or posters, to reinforce the boundaries.

3. Create a Relaxing Atmosphere Design your tech-free sanctuary to be inviting and conducive to relaxation. Use comfortable furniture, calming colors, and natural elements like plants or flowers. Incorporate soft lighting and soothing scents to enhance the ambiance. Dr. Nicholas Carr recommends creating a sensory-rich environment to support relaxation and mindfulness.

4. Incorporate Activities Provide a variety of activities that can be enjoyed in your tech-free sanctuary. These might include reading, journaling, meditation, yoga, or creative hobbies like drawing or knitting. Having designated activities helps reinforce the tech-free nature of the space and provides alternatives to digital engagement.

Additional Tips for Designing Tech-Free Sanctuaries

1. USE ANALOG ALTERNATIVES Replace digital devices with analog alternatives in your tech-free zones. Use physical books, journals, board games, and puzzles to encourage offline engagement. Dr. Sherry Turkle emphasizes the value of tactile experiences for enhancing mindfulness and presence.

2. Schedule Tech-Free Time In addition to creating tech-free spaces, schedule regular tech-free time in your daily routine. This could include tech-free mornings, evenings, or entire days dedicated to disconnecting from digital devices. Consistent tech-free periods help establish a balanced relationship with technology.

3. Practice Mindfulness Incorporate mindfulness practices into your tech-free sanctuary. Engage in activities like meditation, deep breathing, or mindful walking to promote relaxation and mental clarity. Use the time in your tech-free zone to reconnect with yourself and the present moment.

4. Encourage Social Interaction Use tech-free zones to foster meaningful interactions with family and friends. Encourage conversations, shared meals, and group activities that do not involve digital devices. Dr. Sherry Turkle's research highlights the importance of face-to-face interactions for building strong relationships.

5. Monitor and Adjust Regularly assess the effectiveness of your tech-free zones and make adjustments as needed. Solicit feedback from family members or roommates to ensure the spaces meet everyone's needs. Be flexible and open to changes to maintain the relevance and effectiveness of your tech-free sanctuaries.

Do's and Don'ts of Designing Tech-Free Sanctuaries

DO'S:

- **Do identify tech-free zones**: Determine which areas will be designated as tech-free sanctuaries.

- **Do set clear boundaries**: Establish and communicate rules for your tech-free zones to ensure understanding and respect.

- **Do create a relaxing atmosphere**: Design your tech-free sanctuary to be inviting and conducive to relaxation.

- **Do incorporate activities**: Provide a variety of activities that can be enjoyed without digital devices.

- **Do use analog alternatives**: Replace digital devices with physical books, journals, and games to encourage offline engagement.

- **Do schedule tech-free time**: Regularly disconnect from digital devices to establish a balanced relationship with technology.

- **Do practice mindfulness**: Engage in mindfulness practices to promote relaxation and mental clarity in your tech-free sanctuary.

- **Do encourage social interaction**: Use tech-free zones to foster meaningful interactions with family and friends.

- **Do monitor and adjust**: Regularly assess the effectiveness of your tech-free zones and make necessary adjustments.

Don'ts:

- **Don't ignore the need for tech-free zones**: Designating tech-free spaces is essential for reducing digital distractions and promoting well-being.

- **Don't neglect to communicate boundaries**: Ensure that everyone understands and respects the rules of your tech-free zones.

- **Don't overlook the importance of a relaxing atmosphere**: A comfortable and inviting environment supports relaxation and mindfulness.

- **Don't rely solely on digital devices**: Encourage offline engagement by providing analog alternatives in your tech-free sanctuary.

- **Don't forget to schedule tech-free time**: Regularly disconnecting from digital devices is crucial for maintaining balance.

- **Don't skip mindfulness practices**: Incorporate mindfulness activities to enhance relaxation and mental clarity.

- **Don't neglect social interactions**: Use tech-free zones to foster meaningful conversations and connections with others.

- **Don't ignore feedback**: Regularly assess and adjust your tech-free zones to ensure they meet everyone's needs.

FAQ: Designing Tech-Free Sanctuaries

Q: WHAT IS A TECH-FREE sanctuary? A: A tech-free sanctuary is a designated space where digital devices are not allowed, intended to provide a respite from constant connectivity and digital distractions.

Q: How can I create a tech-free sanctuary? A: Identify areas of your home or workspace to designate as tech-free zones, set clear boundaries, create a relaxing atmosphere, and incorporate activities that can be enjoyed without digital devices.

Q: What are the benefits of tech-free zones? A: Tech-free zones can reduce cognitive overload, improve focus, lower stress levels, and promote meaningful interactions and mental clarity.

Q: How can I set clear boundaries for tech-free zones? A: Establish and communicate rules for your tech-free zones, create visual reminders, and ensure everyone understands and respects the boundaries.

Q: What are some analog alternatives to digital devices? A: Analog alternatives include physical books, journals, board games, puzzles, and creative hobbies like drawing or knitting.

Q: Why is it important to schedule tech-free time? A: Scheduling regular tech-free periods helps establish a balanced relationship with technology and provides opportunities to disconnect and recharge.

Q: How can mindfulness practices enhance tech-free zones? A: Mindfulness practices like meditation, deep breathing, and mindful walking promote relaxation and mental clarity in tech-free sanctuaries.

Q: How can I encourage social interactions in tech-free zones? A: Use tech-free zones to foster meaningful conversations, shared meals, and group activities that do not involve digital devices.

Q: How should I monitor and adjust my tech-free zones? A: Regularly assess the effectiveness of your tech-free zones, solicit feedback from family members or roommates, and make necessary adjustments to maintain their relevance and effectiveness.

Case Studies and Examples

SOPHIA'S TECH-FREE Bedroom Sophia, a project manager, struggled with poor sleep quality due to late-night screen time. She designated her bedroom as a tech-free sanctuary and removed all digital devices. Sophia created a relaxing atmosphere with soft lighting, calming colors, and comfortable bedding. She incorporated activities like reading and journaling before bed. These changes improved her sleep quality and helped her unwind more effectively.

John's Tech-Free Dining Room John, a marketing executive, noticed that family meals were often interrupted by digital devices. He designated the dining room as a tech-free zone and communicated this rule to his family. John added a beautiful centerpiece and used soft lighting to create a welcoming atmosphere. Family meals became more focused and enjoyable, fostering better connections and conversations.

Rachel's Tech-Free Morning Routine Rachel, a teacher, started her day feeling overwhelmed by checking emails and social media first thing in the morning. She decided to create a tech-free morning routine, spending the first hour of her day engaging in activities like yoga, meditation, and enjoying a peaceful breakfast. This routine helped Rachel start her day with a clear mind and improved her overall well-being.

Mark's Tech-Free Living Room Mark, a financial analyst, wanted to create a space for relaxation and social interaction without digital distractions. He designated the living room as a tech-free sanctuary, removing all screens and adding comfortable seating, plants, and soft lighting. Mark and his family enjoyed tech-free evenings playing board games, reading, and having meaningful conversations. This practice strengthened their relationships and reduced stress.

Emily's Tech-Free Meditation Space Emily, a customer service representative, created a tech-free meditation space in a corner of her home. She used calming colors, cushions, and a small fountain to create a serene environment. Emily practiced meditation and deep breathing exercises in this space daily, which helped her reduce stress and improve mental clarity. The tech-free sanctuary became her go-to place for relaxation and mindfulness.

Conclusion

DESIGNING TECH-FREE sanctuaries can significantly improve mental clarity, reduce stress, and enhance overall well-being. By identifying tech-free zones, setting clear boundaries, creating a relaxing atmosphere, incorporating activities, and practicing mindfulness, you can create spaces that provide a respite from digital distractions and support a balanced and healthy lifestyle. Implement these strategies to enjoy the benefits of tech-free sanctuaries and foster meaningful interactions with yourself and others.

Chapter 25: Conducting Healthy Online Meetings

T*he Harmonious Circle*

A team leader, frustrated by the chaos of online meetings, asked the master, "How can I conduct online meetings that are productive and healthy for everyone involved?"

The master gathered the team and led them to a quiet clearing. They formed a circle and sat in silence for a moment, feeling the calmness of their surroundings.

The master spoke, "An effective meeting, like this circle, should be balanced and harmonious. Each voice should have space to be heard, and the flow should be natural."

The team leader asked, "How can we achieve this in our online meetings?"

The master replied, "Start with clear intentions and an agenda. Allow each participant time to speak and listen with full presence. Incorporate breaks and respect everyone's time. Create a space where all feel valued and heard, just as in this harmonious circle."

The team leader understood and began implementing these practices in their online meetings, finding that the meetings became more productive and respectful, fostering a healthy environment for all participants.

Introduction

In the era of remote work, online meetings have become a staple of daily business operations. However, virtual meetings can be draining and unproductive if not managed effectively. This chapter explores best practices for conducting healthy online meetings that are productive, engaging, and less tiring.

Understanding the Challenges of Online Meetings

Online meetings, while convenient, come with unique challenges. These include "Zoom fatigue," technical issues, and the lack of non-verbal communication cues. Dr. Gianpiero Petriglieri, an expert in organizational behavior at INSEAD, notes that virtual meetings require more cognitive effort than in-person meetings due to the need to process non-verbal cues through a screen.

Expert Insights and Research

Research from the *Journal of Occupational Health Psychology* indicates that frequent online meetings can lead to increased stress and fatigue. The study suggests that integrating breaks and using effective meeting strategies can mitigate these negative effects.

Dr. Jeremy Bailenson, a professor at Stanford University and director of the Stanford Virtual Human Interaction Lab, has extensively studied the impact of virtual meetings on mental health. His research highlights the phenomenon of "Zoom fatigue," where the constant need to maintain eye contact and interpret non-verbal cues through a screen can be mentally exhausting.

Practical Steps and Tips

1. Set Clear Objectives Before scheduling a meeting, determine whether it is necessary and what you aim to achieve. Clear objectives help keep the meeting focused and productive. Dr. Steven Rogelberg, author of *The Surprising Science of Meetings*, emphasizes the importance of having a clear agenda to avoid unnecessary meetings and ensure that all participants understand the purpose.

2. Keep Meetings Short and Structured Shorter meetings tend to be more effective and less tiring. Aim to keep meetings under 25 minutes whenever possible. Use a structured agenda to guide the discussion and stay on track. Dr. Rogelberg's research suggests that meeting duration is inversely related to productivity; shorter, focused meetings yield better results.

3. Encourage Participation and Engagement Encourage all participants to contribute to the discussion. Use interactive tools like polls, breakout rooms, and collaborative documents to engage attendees. Dr. Ruth Wageman, a researcher on team dynamics, notes that active participation can enhance team cohesion and ensure that diverse perspectives are considered.

4. Integrate Breaks For longer meetings, incorporate short breaks to reduce fatigue. Even a five-minute break can help participants recharge and return to the meeting with renewed focus. Dr. Bailenson's research supports the inclusion of breaks to prevent cognitive overload and maintain engagement.

5. Optimize Your Environment Encourage participants to join meetings from a quiet, well-lit space to minimize distractions and ensure clear communication. Using headphones can improve audio quality and reduce background noise. Dr. Bailenson also recommends minimizing on-screen distractions by closing unnecessary tabs and applications.

Additional Tips for Healthy Online Meetings

1. Use Video Judiciously While video can enhance communication, it can also contribute to fatigue. Encourage participants to use video when necessary but allow them to turn it off during non-essential parts of the meeting. This approach can reduce the pressure to maintain constant eye contact and help participants feel more comfortable.

2. Establish Meeting Etiquette Set ground rules for online meetings, such as muting microphones when not speaking, using the raise hand feature, and avoiding multitasking. Clear etiquette helps maintain order and ensures that everyone has an opportunity to speak.

3. Schedule Meetings Thoughtfully Avoid scheduling back-to-back meetings to give participants time to decompress between sessions. Dr. Petriglieri's research highlights the importance of scheduling breaks between meetings to prevent burnout and improve overall meeting quality.

4. Record Meetings for Later Reference Recording meetings can be useful for participants who are unable to attend or for reviewing key points later. Make sure to inform participants if the meeting will be recorded and provide access to the recording afterward.

5. Evaluate Meeting Effectiveness Regularly assess the effectiveness of your meetings by soliciting feedback from participants. Use this feedback to make improvements and ensure that your meetings remain productive and engaging. Dr. Rogelberg emphasizes the value of continuous improvement in meeting management practices.

Do's and Don'ts of Conducting Healthy Online Meetings
Do's:

• **Do set clear objectives**: Define the purpose of the meeting and communicate it to all participants.

• **Do keep meetings short and structured**: Use a clear agenda and aim to keep meetings under 25 minutes.

• **Do encourage participation and engagement**: Use interactive tools and encourage contributions from all attendees.

• **Do integrate breaks**: Incorporate short breaks in longer meetings to reduce fatigue.

• **Do optimize your environment**: Join meetings from a quiet, well-lit space and use headphones to improve audio quality.

• **Do use video judiciously**: Encourage video use when necessary but allow participants to turn it off during non-essential parts.

• **Do establish meeting etiquette**: Set ground rules for online meetings to maintain order and ensure effective communication.

• **Do schedule meetings thoughtfully**: Avoid back-to-back meetings and schedule breaks between sessions.

• **Do record meetings for later reference**: Inform participants if the meeting will be recorded and provide access to the recording.

• **Do evaluate meeting effectiveness**: Solicit feedback from participants to make continuous improvements.

Don'ts:

- **Don't hold unnecessary meetings**: Ensure that each meeting has a clear purpose and objective.

- **Don't let meetings run too long**: Keep meetings concise and focused to maintain productivity.

- **Don't exclude participants from the discussion**: Encourage contributions from all attendees to ensure diverse perspectives.

- **Don't ignore the need for breaks**: Regular breaks are essential to prevent cognitive overload and maintain engagement.

- **Don't join meetings from noisy or poorly lit environments**: Optimize your environment for clear communication.

- **Don't require video for the entire meeting**: Allow participants to turn off video during non-essential parts to reduce fatigue.

- **Don't ignore meeting etiquette**: Clear ground rules help maintain order and effective communication.

- **Don't schedule back-to-back meetings**: Give participants time to decompress between sessions.

- **Don't forget to record important meetings**: Recording meetings can be useful for participants who are unable to attend or for reviewing key points later.

- **Don't ignore feedback**: Regularly assess the effectiveness of your meetings and make improvements based on participant feedback.

FAQ: Conducting Healthy Online Meetings

Q: How can I set clear objectives for my meetings? A: Define the purpose of the meeting and communicate it to all participants in advance. Use a structured agenda to guide the discussion and stay on track.

Q: How long should online meetings be? A: Aim to keep meetings under 30 minutes whenever possible. Shorter meetings tend to be more effective and less tiring.

Q: How can I encourage participation and engagement? A: Use interactive tools like polls, breakout rooms, and collaborative documents to engage attendees. Encourage all participants to contribute to the discussion.

Q: Why are breaks important in online meetings? A: Incorporating short breaks in longer meetings can help reduce fatigue and maintain engagement. Even a five-minute break can make a difference.

Q: How can I optimize my environment for online meetings? A: Join meetings from a quiet, well-lit space and use headphones to improve audio quality and reduce background noise. Minimize on-screen distractions by closing unnecessary tabs and applications.

Q: Should video be required for all online meetings? A: While video can enhance communication, it can also contribute to fatigue. Encourage participants to use video when necessary but allow them to turn it off during non-essential parts of the meeting.

Q: What are some common meeting etiquette rules? A: Set ground rules such as muting microphones when not speaking, using the raise hand feature, and avoiding multitasking. Clear etiquette helps maintain order and ensures effective communication.

Q: How can I evaluate the effectiveness of my meetings? A: Regularly assess the effectiveness of your meetings by soliciting feedback from participants. Use this feedback to make improvements and ensure that your meetings remain productive and engaging.

Case Studies and Examples

Sophia's Structured Team Meetings Sophia, a team leader at a marketing firm, implemented structured agendas for her online meetings. She set clear objectives for each meeting and encouraged all team members to contribute to the discussion. Sophia also incorporated short breaks in longer meetings to reduce fatigue. These changes led to more focused and productive meetings.

John's Engagement Strategies John, a project manager, used interactive tools like polls and breakout rooms to engage his team during online meetings. He encouraged active participation and ensured that everyone had an opportunity to speak. John's team reported feeling more engaged and motivated during meetings.

Rachel's Meeting Etiquette Rachel, a customer service manager, established clear meeting etiquette for her team. She set ground rules such as muting microphones when not speaking and avoiding multitasking. Rachel also scheduled regular breaks between back-to-back meetings to give her team time to decompress. These practices improved communication and reduced stress during meetings.

Mark's Optimized Environment Mark, a financial analyst, optimized his environment for online meetings by joining from a quiet, well-lit space and using headphones to improve audio quality. He also minimized on-screen distractions by closing unnecessary tabs and applications. Mark found that these adjustments helped him stay focused and engaged during meetings.

Emily's Video Use Policy Emily, a software developer, implemented a flexible video use policy for her team's online meetings. She encouraged video use when necessary but allowed team members to turn it off during non-essential parts of the meeting. Emily's team appreciated the flexibility and reported feeling less fatigued during meetings.

By implementing these best practices, you can conduct healthy online meetings that are productive, engaging, and less draining. Regularly assess and refine your meeting strategies to ensure they continue to meet the needs of your team and yourself!

Sources

1. **American Academy of Ophthalmology**. Recommendations for reducing glare and adjusting screen brightness.

2. **American Optometric Association**. Guidance on the 20-20-20 rule and the use of artificial tears to alleviate dry eyes.

3. **American Psychological Association**. Research on the effects of constant connectivity on stress and anxiety.

4. **Anshel, Dr. Jeff**. Founder of the Ocular Nutrition Society, insights on digital eye strain.

5. **Bloom, Dr. Nicholas**. Research on remote work productivity and well-being.

6. **Cal Newport**. *Digital Minimalism: Choosing a Focused Life in a Noisy World.*

7. **Czeisler, Dr. Charles**. Research on the importance of reducing screen time before bed to improve sleep.

8. **Dunaief, Dr. Joshua**. University of Pennsylvania, emphasizing regular eye exams for screen users.

9. **Forest**. Focus-boosting app that uses virtual trees to encourage users to stay off their phones.

10. **Focus@Will**. Music app designed to improve concentration through scientifically optimized music tracks.

11. **Freedom**. App that blocks distracting websites and apps.

12. **Gazzaley, Dr. Adam**. *The Distracted Mind.*

13. **Gloria Mark, Dr.**. University of California, Irvine, research on attention.

14. **Headspace**. Mindfulness and meditation app offering guided sessions for stress management.

15. **Hedge, Dr. Alan**. Cornell University, research on ergonomic design.

16. **Insight Timer**. App for guided digital mindfulness meditations.

17. **International Data Corporation (IDC)**. Predictions about the growth of the smart home market.

18. **Journal of Behavioral Addictions**. Study on the impact of digital minimalism on mental health and cognitive function.

19. **Journal of Consumer Research**. Research on productivity apps and cognitive load.

20. **Journal of Environmental Psychology**. Research on the impact of digital clutter on mental health and productivity.

21. **Journal of Occupational Health Psychology**. Research on mindfulness practices and cognitive function.

22. **Journal of Social and Clinical Psychology**. Study on the effects of reducing social media use on mental health.

23. **Kondo, Marie**. *The Life-Changing Magic of Tidying Up.*

24. **McKinsey Global Institute**. Report on the impact of productivity tools on efficiency.

25. **Microsoft**. Study on human attention span reduction.

26. **Ostrin, Dr. Lisa**. Research on digital eye strain and the benefits of blue light filters.

27. **Pew Research Center**. Studies on the impact of technology on communication and stress.

28. **Pomodone**. App integrating the Pomodoro Technique with task management.

29. **Sherry Turkle**. *Reclaiming Conversation: The Power of Talk in a Digital Age*.

30. **The Vision Council**. Reports on symptoms of digital eye strain.

31. **Todoist**. Task management app to organize tasks and projects.

32. **Trello**. Visual project management tool.

33. **Turkle, Sherry**. Research on the importance of face-to-face interactions.

34. **Unroll.Me**. Tool for managing email subscriptions.

35. **World Bank**. Study on the impact of access to information on education and economic opportunities.

36. **Harvard Business Review**. Emphasis on the importance of setting boundaries to maintain a healthy work-life balance.

37. **Dr. Nicholas Kardaras**. *Glow Kids: How Screen Addiction Is Hijacking Our Kids—and How to Break the Trance*.

38. **Journal of the Acoustical Society of America**. Study on the impact of ambient noise and interruptions on cognitive performance.

39. **Occupational Safety and Health Administration (OSHA)**. Guidelines for setting up ergonomic workspaces to prevent common injuries.

40. **Dr. Mark Williams**. Co-author of *Mindfulness: A Practical Guide to Finding Peace in a Frantic World*, explains digital mindfulness benefits.

41. **Dr. Jon Kabat-Zinn**. A pioneer in mindfulness, emphasizing its practice in digital interactions.

Don't miss out!

Click the button below and you can sign up to receive emails whenever Eric Porres publishes a new book. There's no charge and no obligation.

Sign Me Up!

https://books2read.com/r/B-A-XHCLB-AXDID

BOOKS 2 READ

Connecting independent readers to independent writers.

About the Author

As the leader of a Logitech innovation group and a former CMO of several successful tech companies, I have witnessed firsthand the profound impact of technology on our lives. I am dedicated to helping you develop smarter wellness habits and achieve a balanced, productive digital lifestyle. This ebook is a culmination of my research, expertise, and passion for promoting digital well-being.

    I hope you find this guide valuable and inspiring. By embracing the principles and practices outlined in this ebook, you can take control of your digital life, enhance your productivity, and improve your overall well-being. Let's embark on this journey together towards a healthier, more balanced relationship with technology.

www.ingramcontent.com/pod-product-compliance
Lightning Source LLC
Chambersburg PA
CBHW050055230526
45470CB00004B/1542